CONTEMP

General Editors

MALCOLM BRADBURY

and

CHRISTOPHER BIGSBY

IRIS MURDOCH

IRIS
MURDOCH

RICHARD TODD

METHUEN
LONDON AND NEW YORK

First published in 1984 by
Methuen & Co. Ltd
11 New Fetter Lane, London EC4P 4EE
Published in the USA by
Methuen & Co.
in association with Methuen, Inc.
733 Third Avenue, New York, NY 10017

© *1984 Richard Todd*

Typeset by Rowland Phototypesetting Ltd
Printed in Great Britain by
Richard Clay (The Chaucer Press) Ltd
Bungay, Suffolk

British Library Cataloguing in Publication Data

Todd, Richard
Iris Murdoch. – (Contemporary writers)
1. Murdoch, Iris – Criticism and interpretation
I. Title   II. Series
823'.914   PR6063.SU7Z/

ISBN 0-416-35420-3

Library of Congress Cataloging in Publication Data

Todd, Richard.
Iris Murdoch.
(Contemporary writers)
Bibliography: p.
1. Murdoch, Iris, – Criticism and interpretation.
I. Title.   II. Series.
PR6063.U7Z924   1984   823'914   84-1155
ISBN 0-416-35420-3 (pbk.)

CONTENTS

GENERAL EDITORS' PREFACE

The contemporary is a country which we all inhabit, but there is little agreement as to its boundaries or its shape. The serious writer is one of its most sensitive interpreters, but criticism is notoriously cautious in offering a response or making a judgement. Accordingly, this continuing series is an endeavour to look at some of the most important writers of our time, and the questions raised by their work. It is, in effect, an attempt to map the contemporary, to describe its aesthetic ànd moral topography.

The series came into existence out of two convictions. One was that, despite all the modern pressures on the writer and on literary culture, we live in a major creative time, as vigorous and alive in its distinctive way as any that went before. The other was that, though criticism itself tends to grow more theoretical and apparently indifferent to contemporary creation, there are grounds for a lively aesthetic debate. This series, which includes books written from various standpoints, is meant to provide a forum for that debate. By design, some of those who have contributed are themselves writers, willing to respond to their contemporaries; others are critics who have brought to the discussion of current writing the spirit of contemporary criticism or simply a conviction, forcibly and coherently argued, for the contemporary significance of their subjects. Our aim, as the series develops, is to continue to explore the works of major post-war writers — in fiction, drama and poetry – over an international range, and thereby to illuminate not only those works but also in some degree the artistic, social and moral assumptions on which they rest. Our wish is that, in their very variety of approach and emphasis, these books will stimulate interest in and understanding of the vitality of a living literature which, because it is contemporary, is especially ours.

Norwich, England

MALCOLM BRADBURY
CHRISTOPHER BIGSBY

ACKNOWLEDGEMENTS

Iris Murdoch's readers are many and international. Yet one has only to read the reviews of each new addition to her extensive *œuvre* to realize that there is a great deal of uncertainty about the kind of novelist she is, and about the kind of imaginative enquiry which her books develop. This book is an attempt to answer these questions. Iris Murdoch commented discerningly on an early outline of this undertaking, but it must not of course be assumed that she necessarily endorses everything which it contains; she has been characteristically generous in correspondence. During an extremely busy semester, my colleagues in the *Vakgroep Engelse Letterkunde* (Department of English Literature) at the Vrije Universiteit, Amsterdam, agreed to release me from teaching and other duties; their kindness greatly facilitated my work on this project, and the book is offered to them with many thanks. For comment and assistance whether recently or in the past, I should also like to thank Christopher Bigsby, Antonia Byatt, Michel Le Cat, Peter Conradi, August Fry, Mike Hannay, Katherine Manville, Janice Price, Winnie Todd and, especially, Malcolm Bradbury, who made many cogent and helpful suggestions, and John Fletcher, who generously allowed me to consult the material of his forthcoming *Iris Murdoch: A Descriptive Primary and Annotated Secondary Bibliography* (New York: Garland). I am grateful to the editors of the *Dutch Quarterly Review* for letting me draw on my article, 'The Plausibility of *The Black*

Prince', first published in their pages in 1978, and to the staff at Chatto & Windus Ltd, who patiently answered enquiries and allowed me access to material in their possession.

The author and publisher would like to thank the following for permission to reproduce copyright material: Iris Murdoch, Chatto & Windus Ltd and Viking Penguin, Inc. for extracts from the novels of Iris Murdoch; Iris Murdoch and J. M. Dent & Sons Ltd for an extract from *Black Paper 1975*, edited by C. B. Cox and Rhodes Boyson.

Amsterdam, The Netherlands, 1984   RICHARD TODD

A NOTE ON THE TEXTS

Page references for quotations from Iris Murdoch's books are to the British Triad/Panther editions, unless otherwise stated. The following abbreviations have been used:

Sa	*Sartre: Romantic Rationalist* (London; Fontana/Collins, 1967
UTN	*Under the Net*
FFE	*The Flight from the Enchanter*
S	*The Sandcastle*
B	*The Bell*
ASH	*A Severed Head*
UR	*An Unofficial Rose* (Harmondsworth; Penguin, 1964)
U	*The Unicorn*
IG	*The Italian Girl* (Harmondsworth; Penguin, 1971)
RG	*The Red and the Green*
TA	*The Time of the Angels* (Harmondsworth; Penguin, 1968)
NG	*The Nice and the Good*
BD	*Bruno's Dream*
FHD	*A Fairly Honourable Defeat* (Harmondsworth; Penguin, 1972)
AM	*An Accidental Man* (Harmondsworth; Penguin, 1973)
BP	*The Black Prince* (Harmondsworth; Penguin, 1975)
SPLM	*The Sacred and Profane Love Machine* (Harmondsworth; Penguin, 1976)

WC	*A Word Child*
HC	*Henry and Cato*
TSTS	*The Sea, The Sea*
NS	*Nuns and Soldiers*
PP	*The Philosopher's Pupil* (London: Chatto & Windus, 1983)

1

INTRODUCTION

To assert that Iris Murdoch is a major contemporary writer is
to suggest something of the state of the post-war novel in
Britain. In the period since the appearance of her first published
novel *Under the Net* in 1954, she has emerged not only as one
of the most productive and influential British novelists of her
generation but, equally importantly, as a powerfully intellectual and original theorist of fiction. The increasingly evident
liveliness and variety of British fiction since the war has contrasted very curiously with a sense of restraint about aesthetic
discussion of the novel: Iris Murdoch is unusual in having
consistently taken a clear view of the form she has explored.
She has emphasized that she aims to write as a realist, in an
identifiably nineteenth-century tradition of English and European fiction. At the same time, however, she has maintained
that it is now practically impossible for novelists to do this, for
good philosophical and epistemological reasons. In all this, she
has indicated the difficulties and at the same time the potential
of contemporary fiction, especially in the British tradition, and
both her views and her practice are deeply revealing about the
novel today.

Nor can her readers avoid the debate. To some, it seems as
though her novel-writing career enacts a retreat into the safety
of an anti-modernist position; such readers find it hard to
accept the large claims she advances, in an age of aesthetic and
epistemological uncertainty, for the continuing accessibility of

the nineteenth-century 'greats' (Tolstoy, Dostoevsky, Dickens) and – lying behind their achievement – Shakespeare, whom she has more than once described as the 'patron saint' of novelists. To others, her traditional stance offers an extraordinarily invigorating and articulate challenge to the prevalent ideas which, since the war, have been rather more characteristic of the novel in the United States and France than in Britain: that the novel can survive only through radical experiment, that it must manifest linguistic and formal daring, that attention to concepts such as 'character' and 'narrative' should be replaced by phenomenological concerns, mediated by a detached linguistic scrupulousness, and that humanistic realism is no longer a ready option for fiction.

Murdoch's theoretical position is in fact a deeply examined one. It owes its development not simply to her 'other' career as one of Britain's leading moral philosophers, but results, more generally, from a habit of reading and thought which displays a carefully cultivated, historically aware, and genuinely international literary sensibility (unlike that of other writers who have been associated with the revival of realism in post-war Britain). It arises from strong conceptions of the role of art in society and as an instrument of human knowledge. We have to grant her convictions about the humanistic value of nineteenth-century realism and the importance of realizing 'character' in the contemporary novel at the same time as, for instance, grasping the extent of her acquaintance with essential currents in the intellectual life of post-war France, appreciating her early – and at the time unfashionable – championing of the work of Elias Canetti, and sharing her sympathy for the fiction of contemporary exponents of 'fantasy realism', such as Gabriel Garcia Márquez. We have also to be able to read her novels less as examples of traditional realism than as manifestations of curiosity about the elements and assumptions which made the novel a serious form of art, in so far as they constitute an extended enquiry which has itself deepened and grown complex as time has gone by. In this way her career can be seen to have fallen into a number of phases and stages leading her from the influence of post-war existentialist fiction to a position now peculiarly her own.

*

Iris Murdoch was born of Anglo-Irish parents in Dublin in 1919, although she was brought up in London, in Hammersmith and Chiswick, and only returned to Ireland during childhood for holidays. The landscape of her fiction largely reflects these facts. Her Anglo-Irish background has given her a distinct sense of bi-national identity, and it has certainly fed the striking topography of her fiction. Place is always important to her novels, but Irish settings occur in works which are perhaps least central to her achievement – from the early short story 'Something Special' (1957) to her one specifically historical novel, *The Red and the Green* (1965), set in the Irish troubles of 1916. More characteristic is the transmutation of Irish materials into the atmospheric, Gothic environments of *The Unicorn* (1963) or *The Sea, The Sea* (1978). When topographic specificity is strong, this more usually means a British setting, and mainly one in the south or south Midlands, though the elaborately defined southern spa town of *The Philosopher's Pupil* (1983) takes us somewhat further afield. Yet all these settings are recognizably 'Murdochland': London especially is important to her books, but it is a very particular London, usually the inner south-western sections of Brompton, Hammersmith, Chelsea, Kensington, Notting Hill and the region round the Post Office tower, those parts of London that Jake Donaghue in *Under the Net* calls 'necessary' rather than 'contingent'.

About her childhood, Murdoch stresses two things: that she grew up without siblings and that it was happy. She began writing fiction at a tender age; she was educated at the Froebel Institute, then at Badminton School near Bath, after which she went to Somerville College, Oxford. Here, like many other intellectuals during the 1930s, she became a member of the Communist Party; she later resigned in disillusion, but remained for a long time close to the Left. After graduating in

Classics, she followed her father into the Civil Service, entering the Treasury in 1942 as an Assistant Principal. There was now a sustained period of novel writing during which five books were written before *Under the Net* was published in 1954; one was submitted to Faber but rejected, and has not appeared since. Wishing to play a more active part in the war, Murdoch left the Treasury in 1944 to join the wartime relief operation, UNRRA (United Nations Relief and Rehabilitation Administration), working with refugees in Belgium and Austria. Her time in Brussels was of particular importance to her intellectual life and direction; it was here that she first encountered the existentialist movement, which was to have such importance in the redirection of wartime and post-war philosophy both on the continent and in Britain. She was one of the earliest non-Gallic readers of Jean-Paul Sartre's *L'Etre et le Néant* (1943), and met its author in 1945; his philosophical theories and literary achievement formed the subject of her own first published book, *Sartre: Romantic Rationalist* (1953). The book acknowledges Sartre's deepened portrait of consciousness, the parallelisms between existentialist and British philosophy, and also the importance of the novel as a mode of human enquiry:

> The novel is a picture of, and a comment upon, the human condition, and a typical product of the era to which belong also the writings of Nietzsche, the psychology of Freud, the philosophy of Sartre. It is also a type of writing which is more important, in the sense of being more influential, than any of the last mentioned. (*Sa*, p. 10)

Sartre's influence on Murdoch is complex; it is primarily philosophical and political, though she has expressed great admiration for the more literary aspects of his writing. Even so, his novels have not influenced her fiction as widely as is sometimes thought, despite her admiration for his most perfect novel, *La Nausée* (1938), and the indubitable, if fleeting, echoes of that book in *Under the Net*. Existentialist readings have been offered of several of her books, often overemphasizing the impact of this in any case very heterodox philosophical movement; and Sartre's intention of being a 'philosophical novelist' has also been attributed to Murdoch. But what is perhaps more important is that in the disturbing intellectual years at the end of the war Murdoch felt the influence of ideas which essentially changed the prevailing portraits of consciousness, challenged our views of human nature and human freedom, altered the portrait of the relation of individual to society and 'self' to 'other', and questioned the nature of language and communication. Murdoch's subsequent arguments about realism, literature and art undoubtedly have their origins in many of these issues, but the reinterpretation is distinctive, and there is in fact an increasing detachment from Sartre as time goes on.

Much the same might be said about the impact of two other writers influential on her literary development during the late 1940s and 1950s, Samuel Beckett and Raymond Queneau. Regarding Sartre, Murdoch challenged his development, feeling that the greater flexibility his 'literariness' gave to all his earlier work disappeared in his later, *engagé* phase. Dating her acquaintance with Beckett's *Murphy* (1938) to the beginning of the Second World War, she has repeatedly declared herself puzzled by his movement towards literary and philosophical minimalism, as by his decision to cease writing exclusively in English; and more recently she has confessed to admiring his work as a whole less than she used to. Beckett shows his influence in *Under the Net* but it is to Raymond Queneau that the book is dedicated. Here she has said she prefers the bizarrely peripatetic quality of the less well-known novels of the 1930s and 1940s to works like *Zazie dans le Métro* (1959) or the exercises in style which brought Queneau to the notice of English-speaking readers. And *Under the Net* seems to show some imprint from a book such as *Pierrot mon Ami* (1943) – in particular a scene where Pierrot is commissioned to travel with some circus animals (this is so treated that only gradually do we realize that his companions are not human) bears some relation to the Mister Mars episodes of Murdoch's novel – and

17

Queneau's surrealistically unjudging attitude has some relation to her tone. But in general all these influences were strongest at the beginning of Murdoch's career, and although *Under the Net* is still high in critical esteem, Murdoch has more than once spoken of it as a derivative and juvenile book. Certainly there were considerable changes thereafter in both her work and her philosophical attitude, and in her notion of the capacities of the novel.

Shortly after the war, on account of her one-time membership of the Communist Party, Murdoch was refused a visa to the United States; this would have allowed her to take up a scholarship in philosophy, which she had now decided to study academically. After she left UNRRA in 1946 a less settled but formative period followed, spent reading and thinking in both London and Europe. To this time must doubtless be attributed the acquisition of at least some of the impressive topographical knowledge deployed in *Under the Net* and elsewhere, and the impressively sure philosophical knowledge deployed in *Sartre*, her essays and her novels. From 1947 to 1948 she held the Sarah Smithson studentship in philosophy at Newnham College, Cambridge, and came under new influences. Though she was not formally taught by Ludwig Wittgenstein, she did meet him, and, as she has recently put it, 'lived, in terms of philosophy, in the aura of his work'.[1] During this time, besides collecting material for *Sartre*, she was continuing to write fiction. In 1948 she returned to Oxford as Fellow and Tutor in Philosophy at St Anne's College, where, on ceasing tutorial work in 1963, she became an Honorary Fellow. In 1956 she married the writer and literary critic John Bayley, now Professor of English at Oxford, whose literary criticism offers some illumination of her work. After 1963, although by now a very successful and widely read novelist, she continued to teach philosophy part-time in London, holding a post at the Royal College of Art until 1967 and teaching at University College. Though she has subsequently found it impossible to continue with a regular teaching post, she has remained closely in contact with the academic world, undertaking lecture tours, publishing philosophical work, and participating in the British intellectual scene to a degree nowadays unusual among writers.

Meanwhile her work has achieved ever increasing recognition. *Under the Net* was warmly acclaimed, but somewhat misunderstood, and seen as part of the so-called Movement associated with the work of the 'Angry Young Men'. Murdoch's evident existential interests made it easy to link the book with the work of a generation of new writers writing from new class backgrounds with a new social topography, and in revolt against previous social fiction and experimental modernism. But, as many critics, including Blake Morrison, have subsequently stressed, the affinities being looked for here were not at all strong.[2] From the 1950s onward her productive flow of novels held continuous public attention as the work of no other post-war British novelist has quite succeeded in doing. In the 1960s the very frequency of her novels seemed to earn her some critical hostility, although it was also in this period that A. S. Byatt's important, understanding study of her early novels, *Degrees of Freedom* (1965), appeared. The later 1960s saw a change of direction: the length of her novels increased and their tone altered, though the rate of production – which had become more or less annual – did not slow down appreciably. But this was mature work, displaying what her more serious admirers had long sensed: her uncompromisingly firm grasp of the intellectual demands of literary form. The 1970s began to see public recognition of her achievement. She was elected to the Irish Academy in 1970 and became an Honorary Member of the American Academy of Arts and Letters in 1975; in 1977 she was made Honorary Fellow of her old college, Somerville. Her novels won increasing honours: *The Black Prince* was awarded the James Tait Black Memorial Prize in 1973, *The Sacred and Profane Love Machine* the Whitbread Literary Award in 1974. But it was not until 1978 that due acclamation came when, after being more than once runner-up, she was awarded Britain's most prestigious literary award, the Booker-McConnell Prize, for *The Sea, The Sea*. By now her reputation was international. In 1961 it was already being noted that, at the height of the cold war, she was one of the few contemporary British novelists being widely read in the Soviet Union, although not until 1966 was *Under the Net* translated into Russian (three more novels have followed since). *Under the Net* indeed remains her most translated book (virtually the entire canon is in Danish and Dutch; more than three-quarters of her fiction is in French, Spanish, Swedish and Japanese).[3] Murdochland is now an internationally known landscape and the direction of her fiction represents a significant tendency of the contemporary British novel.

*

But if no living British novelist has held public attention since the 1950s in the way that Irish Murdoch has, and although her reputation has never been more secure, it is apparent from the reviews her work receives that its substance and spirit still remain elusive. Although the novels of the 1960s were received the least favourably, there had been some adverse comment in the 1950s: then it was maintained that her work was too cerebral (the comparison with Aldous Huxley was made frequently and from an early date) or too detachedly ironic; more recently we have heard complaints of her blandness (Angela Carter) or her self-indulgence and stylistic laxness (Christopher Ricks, John Updike). There are some who see her novels primarily as high-flown sentimental romances, others who read in them a great moral urgency and an intense artistic self-awareness. Those critics of the 1950s who read her as an Angry Young Man must be set off against those who saw her as Britain's version of the French philosophical novelist. Her own critical theory has been very variously read: as a defence of nineteenth-century realist practices in fiction, and as a form of pressing contemporaneity which must possess what she read in Jean-Paul Sartre: 'he has the style of the age' (*Sa* p. 7). The elusiveness indeed seems part of her very conception of the novel. The distrust of endings and completeness in art, which her work has always implicitly conveyed and has come more explicitly to show, is reflected in the manner in which each novel has been *despatched* in order to make way for the next. And though this has prompted some critical censure of the hurriedness of some of the work, it does allow Murdoch to be seen as she seems to want to be seen – as constantly working at a form she takes with great seriousness.

Closing her book on Sartre in 1953, Murdoch seemed there to assert the difficulties of the contemporary novel as they appeared to her. The novel, she said, is 'properly an art of image rather than of analysis', and Sartre was the novelist as rationalist:

> His passion both to possess a big theoretical machine and to gear it on to the details of practical activity compares favourably with the indifference of those who are complacently content to let history get on without them. His inability to write a great novel is a tragic symptom of a situation which afflicts us all. We know that the real lesson to be taught is that the human person is precious and unique; but we seem unable to set it forth except in terms of ideology and abstraction. (*Sa*, pp. 119–20)

She seems to call for the novelist as philosopher, but not the philosophical novelist. She returned to this issue in reviewing Simone de Beauvoir's novel *The Mandarins* in 1957, noticing the book's crucial theme, that of freedom and the contradictions of liberalism, and observing that it is 'a remarkable book, a novel on the grand scale, courageous in its exactitude and endearing because of its persistent seriousness'. Yet at the same time we are starved of the power of imagination:

> We are struck by the absence of the novelist's traditional furniture: social institutions, customs, the moral virtues. There is no steady and opaque framework. The characters take nothing for granted, and their encounters take place in a sort of social and intellectual State of Nature.[4]

In the interest and the dissent seem to lie some of the more significant driving forces of Murdoch's fiction. De Beauvoir's novels, like Sartre's, are *engagé*; of Murdoch it has often been remarked that, for a thinker of definitely radical if no longer unquestionably left-wing instincts, there is surprisingly little political commitment in her novels. And although she admired such commitment in the novels of Sartre and de Beauvoir, she sees this as a central issue in discussion of their work, a primary challenge which she must redefine. As a result she has, for herself, a very clear sense of restraint about the relationship between politically committed and creative fictional writing.

This evidently has much to do with her sense of the novel's specificity and its value as a distinctive form of understanding. For more explicit political comment than we find in her novels, we may look to her drama; she regards her talents and intentions as unsuited to such explicitness in fiction. The closest she has ever really come to writing a 'political' novel results in something very different from *Les Chemins de la Liberté*. Her second novel, *The Flight from the Enchanter* (1956), is, by the standards of her later fiction, a busy, frequently fantastic work, but there is some sustained attention given to the fate of the political refugee, and – though nostalgically, through a group of elderly suffragettes – to women's rights. The first of these matters recurs in the later fiction – the middle-European, if not actually Polish or Russian, *émigré* is a familiar figure in the Murdoch canon – and she clearly feels a constant need to attend to such instances of modern displacement, a need which she has linked with her own background and her experiences with UNRRA. As to women's rights, Murdoch, it must be said, shows no interest in radical feminism as such, and has several times said that her interest in women's liberation is a non-militant one that extends into more general concerns, especially those affecting education. She considers there is a good deal of powerful if subdued political comment in all her novels. A firm believer in the power of the political pamphlet, she has written on issues such as homosexuality, Vietnam (she strongly condemned American intervention), nuclear weapons and school education (opposing indiscriminate comprehensivization of schools in Britain). Several of these topics do arise in her novels, particularly in the 1970s, and in their presentation we may sense a Sartrean existentialist concern for advocating freedom of human action, a freedom which is located firmly in the context of those complexities that inevitably arise when the individual's predicament within society is considered. Her general outlook in this and other respects also owes much to the thought of Simone Weil.

But the *engagé* novel is not explicitly her aim or purpose. Her idiosyncratically fabulistic understanding of social realism requires that in fiction an individual be presented with the utmost specificity against the background of a real and dynamic picture of human society. This is the political person's problem, the philosopher's and above all the writer's; the novel requires a 'steady and opaque framework'. The amount of specificity will be a function of the writer's moral ability to create character. Under ideal circumstances of ability, commitment and historical context, such presentation will avoid what Murdoch sees as the real danger of 'rigidity' in fiction. She quarrels with the prescriptive sentimentalism of a good deal of critical reading of literature (that of the illiberal orthodox Marxist analysis of literature, for example), much as she does with F. R. Leavis's prescriptive orthodoxy. Dickens is a test case: Murdoch sees far more realized social awareness and feeling in the figure of Joe, the street-sweeper in *Bleak House* (1853), than in the whole of *Hard Times* (1854), the 'committed' novel Leavis admired, which for her lacks a sense of 'magic' and mysterious impenetrability.[5] As she made clear in her famous essay 'Against Dryness' (1961), she considers that the novel must create essential images of humanity, and must therefore be 'a fit house for free characters to live in'. This involves an essential celebration of the creative imagination, as a moral, ethical and apprehensive power, responding to contradiction and otherness.

In the same sense, she is not quite the 'philosophical novelist' many of her early readers expected her to be. She maintains that philosophy and fiction writing are separate activities, and that in her case the former is subordinate to the latter. Indeed her theory of fiction itself takes issue with the philosophical novel, at any rate that of Sartre's type, where poetry alone is free for the imagination, but prose is committed irrevocably to history. In her book on him she says this explicitly: 'Sartre seems blind to the function of prose, not as an activity or an analytic tool, but as creative of a complete and unclassifiable image' (*Sa*, p. 118). The image must not, she has said, be 'crystalline' or clearly perfected. But if it is surrounded by contingency it is not quite Sartre's contingency: in her world 'whatever is contingent, messy, boundless, infinitely particular, and endlessly still to be explained'[6] holds crucial place. She has also urged that art is a pursuit of the good, which is of itself a form of attention to the particular. The paradox of Plato – that of the philosopher who, dismissing the artist from his republic, proclaims himself by his very thought and writing an artist – has always interested her, and since the publication of her monograph *The Fire and the Sun* in 1977 the theme has proved a real source of speculative fascination for her. A remarkably ceremonious confidence in her own ability to hold the two activities distinct must have been involved in creating the relationship enshrined in the title of her twenty-first novel, *The Philosopher's Pupil*. It is a book explicit in its deployment of recurrent Murdoch types and situations, although in discussion of it she has denied both that she made philosophy its subject in order to express any of her own philosophical viewpoints or theories, and that she intended to set philosophy in opposition to art in it.[7] She prefers to see Rozanov's profession in the novel as consistent with a certain moral absoluteness, which leads to uncompromising and even absurd behaviour in relation to other human beings. She explains his behaviour – as she accounts for the total endeavour of a certain kind of philosopher – in terms of its being an exercise in power, an attempt to master the complexities which must surround the philosophical mind. Rozanov is haunted by the impossibility of ever 'getting it right'.

And all this Murdoch sees in terms of its implications for the novelist's essential task, which is that of creating character by revealing secret obsessions which 'real people' do not give away. It is this understanding which accounts for her complex conception of realism. Today, as we survey the thirty years of Murdoch's novel-writing career, and the still longer period of considered yet intensely eclectic intellectual development related to it, it can only seem to us that she has entered obliquely and indirectly the stream of realism in which she aims to write. Even *The Philosopher's Pupil*, with its detailed discursiveness, contains a number of flamboyant and fantastic set-piece episodes which seem to flaunt their independence of the general context and constitute something essential in her particular voice. The novelist who has rightly been called a 'fabulator' by Robert Scholes is not creating an innocent realism: the thinker who has acknowledged the limitations of the liberal's portrait of the world is not bound by empirical conventions. Murdoch-land, always specific in its topography, has, over the process of Murdoch's writing, constantly moved towards fascinating new definition; in so doing it has drawn attention to the increasingly opaque relationship between its ritual conventions and its author's own mental landscape. To see how this has evolved, we should begin with a closer examination of what Murdoch was bringing to British fiction in the 1950s.

2

'UNDER THE NET'
TO 'THE BELL'

Iris Murdoch's first four published novels can be seen to constitute as distinct a phase as any to be found in her work. They all belong to the 1950s, the time of her strongest interest in the implications of existentialism. They all appeared in quick succession – but the three-year pause after the fourth, *The Bell* (1958), has not since been exceeded in her career. To that pause (1958–61) between *The Bell* and *A Severed Head* (1961) belongs the publication of some of Murdoch's major theoretical work on fiction, including her best-known essay, 'Against Dryness', first published in *Encounter* in January 1961. It is hard to resist the deduction that *The Bell* does conclude a phase in Murdoch's novel-writing *œuvre*, after which she turned her attention to theoretical matters of pressing concern before going on to develop her fiction in a somewhat fresh direction.

Under the Net (1954) remains a formidable début. Even though, in the manner of many established novelists, Murdoch now considers it derivative, it is accomplished enough to be free of the almost inescapably solipsistic flavour and limited range of human experience usual in so many first novels. It is a genuinely European novel, with wide literary debts; it is also certainly a novel of its time, its central character an 'outsider' figure, its form a tale of picaresque adventure – a form itself raising questions about the way in which 'necessary' and 'contingent' elements go into the making of novels. This theme may have encouraged its warm press, but also caused some misunderstanding of its emphasis; it certainly led her work to be associated with the group of new writers of fiction who emerged forcefully in Britain in the early 1950s and have exerted a powerful influence on the direction taken by British fiction since, from Angus Wilson to Kingsley Amis. These connections linked the book with the strong contemporary interest in a new social realism and with the problems of generational and existential self-definition in the new post-war Britain. Its impersonation of a male narrator also helped in the link, although that is probably best seen as an uncompromising exercise in the attainment of 'otherness'. Jake Donaghue, an impecunious and *déraciné* hack translator of the best-selling French writer Jean-Pierre Breteuil, returns from Paris to London in time to learn that the relationship with the girl whose flat he and his companion Finn have been using has come to an end. Faced with the immediate needs of shelter and survival, Jake contemplates the prospect of renewing an earlier friendship, with the singer and actress Anna Quentin. In tracking Anna down to the mime theatre where she now works, Jake is brought back into contact with other people from his past – notably Anna's sister, Sadie, and Hugo Belfounder, a type who appears in several novels, and is Jake's intellectual *alter ego* as well as an apparent sexual rival. Jake's predicament is complicated by his feeling that he had earlier betrayed Hugo by publishing a book called *The Silencer*, which adapts many of their former conversations on language and philosophical matters.

It is from one of these conversations that the novel's title is taken. Murdoch has described Hugo as 'a sort of non-philosophical metaphysician who is supposed to be paralysed in a way by [the] problem' about which the novel plays. As she told Frank Kermode in a 'House of Fiction' interview, the book

plays with a philosophical idea. The problem which is mentioned in the title is the problem of how far conceptu-alizing and theorizing, which from one point of view are absolutely essential, in fact divide you from the thing which is the object of theoretical attention.[8]

The suggestion here seems to be that as literature itself fleshes out that which philosophy might concern itself with, so in the story issues of the relationship between abstract impressions and real experiences are important. And the elusiveness of the real guides the quest structure of the book, which is in fact a double one. In company with Finn and Dave Gellman, Jake seeks intellectual fulfilment in the form of some obscurely planned reconciliation with Hugo in London: in solitude, he seeks erotic fulfilment through his search for Anna, who has, he discovers, left for Paris. The quests dovetail into each other. Jake goes to Paris but does not find Anna; he returns to London, but before he can follow a course of action that will eventually lead him to Hugo, he undergoes a spiritual crisis which seems to owe much to Murdoch's understanding of Sartrean *mauvaise foi*. After some comic financial reverses involving his ex-girlfriend and her bookmaker consort, money becomes his chief need, so with characteristic lack of reflection he takes a job as a hospital cleaner. Now resemblances to Beckett's *Murphy* declare themselves more markedly (the book is earlier said to be among Jake's possessions). Hugo is brought in with a head-wound sustained at a political rally, and Jake, in an obsessive act of reparation, enters the hospital at night. His ensuing conversation with Hugo surely recalls the nocturnal chess game, also rendered in provocative specificity, between Murphy and Mr Endon in the Magdalen Mental Mercyseat.

Among much else in this conversation, Jake learns that his misgivings about *The Silencer* are unfounded; more unsettlingly, he discovers that his unreflective vanity has produced a complete misunderstanding of the circle of unrequited erotic attention in which he and Hugo have been involved with the two Quentin sisters. His emotional world-picture is transformed as he realizes that it is Sadie, and not Anna, who has been in love with him; this affects his attitudes towards words and writing, producing a recovery of specificity and a new attitude towards creativity. The relationship between Hugo and Jake is in fact of a kind recurrent in Murdoch, displaying a conflict she has always seen between two types of writer (or artist). Compared with Hugo, the type of artist represented by Jake is the facile maker of forms, the dealer in apprehensible shapes. Hugo, however, is, as Murdoch has recently phrased it, a type of 'the truthful, formless figure',[9] a person so daunted by the problems of artistic expression that he may in the end remain silent. And Murdoch's very complex relationship with the intellectual awareness manifest in this contrast is a central theme in her work. Time and again, the plots of her fictions contemplate it. Most epigrammatically formulated, it is the contrast between artist and saint, and *Hamlet* is its supreme exemplar. For Murdoch, this can be seen as a play concerning a man's heroic inability to submit to the conventional forms of expression which are available to, and demanded by, his predicament. As a work of art and as a psychologically realistic study of human specificity, which elicits behaviour incompatible with the completeness which characterizes art, the play becomes her paradigm. Here the Shakespearian allusion is so indirect as to be probably still an unconscious influence; it will become far more explicit in her later work. What she has emphasized here is the contrast between 'the man who's silent and the man who speaks; the man who's unconsciously good and the man who's consciously, aesthetically, creating his life . . . a kind of struggle between an angel and a mortal.'[10]

Early reviewers of *Under the Net* were prolix in their comparisons, reading affinities with Cocteau, the Marx brothers, the Crazy Gang, Joyce Cary, Henry Green, E. M. Forster, Kafka and Dostoevsky. But the fruitful comparisons remain with Beckett and the dedicatee, Raymond Queneau. Queneau's own surrealistic understanding of realism owes much to his famous use of *argot*, stimulated by a realization of the difference between ancient and demotic Greek. But if Murdoch admires this, as she admires the powers of Nabokov and Beckett to animate English prose,[11] the larger debt is to the effortlessly humorous texture of Queneau's early work, beneath which a philosophical seriousness is concealed. In this, there are affinities with Simone Weil, whom Murdoch also admires; thus in Queneau's experimental *Le Chiendent* (1933) the notion of 'attention' plays an important part; in this novel one of the characters, all of whom are initially portrayed as silhouettes, achieves a named, substantive presence, as Etienne, once he has attended to a window-display he has failed to notice despite having walked past it for several years. But the amusement-park milieu of *Pierrot mon Ami* and the peripatetic behaviour of the hero seem to be recalled in *Under the Net* in various silent tributes: the rich evocations of theatrical props and the film set, the search for the elusive Anna through Paris. And Pierrot himself, a Dostoevskyan divine fool, is a version of a type that has interested Murdoch greatly. Pierrot's adventures conclude with nothing really having been achieved; they have been worth it because they have happened. A comparable comic resignation occurs at the end of *Under the Net*, where Jake's adventures seem accorded contingent rather than necessary value. The book's epigraph from Dryden's 'Secular Masque' makes exquisite sense in this light:

> All, all of a piece throughout;
> Thy Chase had a Beast in view:
> Thy Wars brought nothing about;
> Thy Lovers were all untrue.
> 'Tis well an old Age is out,
> And time to begin a New.

As the comparisons suggest, *Under the Net* is something more complex than conventional realism. Readers have been impressed by the detailed accuracy of the descriptions of London and Paris during Jake's adventures, but Murdoch herself has been almost cavalierly dismissive of this quality, referring to it as 'self-indulgence' and as 'not [having] any particular significance'.[12] Yet this masks an important distinction between the treatments of the two cities. *Under the Net*'s surreal dimension is most in evidence in the Paris scenes where Jake pursues Anna against the background of the Bastille Day celebrations on 14 July. This quest is obsessively and erotically single-minded, unlike the London quest, where Jake reveals a disarmingly feckless ability to be distracted from the task in hand, the pursuit of Hugo. He likes to see this kind of behaviour as characteristic not of himself but of Finn; Finn's determined action at the end of the story in returning to Dublin is thus a comic reversal that forces Jake at last to pay due attention to him as well. The London scenes are landscaped with a quotidian accuracy, but the action through them is hardly realistic, and one must say of the events in both cities that – as in dream experience – much energy is spent in activities and actions whose significance seems disproportionately small. In a writer with a less sure sense of timing, episodes such as the attempt to get the dog Mister Mars out of his cage, or Jake's tactics for entering the hospital at night, could easily become tedious. Yet here, as elsewhere in early Murdoch, contingent social detail is used in a prolix way, as it is not in, say, *The Bell*; excitement and tension are felt, as in a dream, to be creatively invigorating even though there seems no rational need for them.

Murdoch is here still learning to balance the equation by which she sets much store: 'to combine form with a respect for reality with all its odd contingent ways is the highest art of prose'.[13] It cannot be pretended that *Under the Net* is faultless, though its confidently episodic nature seems flawed only in the light of what is to follow in Murdoch's work. Thus when Jake, his quest over, returns to Hugo's flat and finds he has gone to Nottingham to become a watchmaker, he discovers, first, Hugo's lightly annotated copy of *The Silencer*, then, by breaking open the safe, Anna's letters to Hugo. They fascinate him, yet there is no explanation for his refusal to keep them beyond his saying: 'it was impossible. They were burning my hand' (*UTN*, p. 242). The problem, in its general nature a recurrent one in Murdoch, is that Jake's actions seem to derive less from his character than from an authorial solicitation; the driving compulsiveness seems less Jake's than Murdoch's own. And this tugs against that urgency of 'otherness' which is perhaps the book's basic premise, felt by Jake so sharply at the end:

> It seemed as if, for the first time, Anna really existed now as a separate being and not as part of myself. To experience this was extremely painful. Yet as I tried to keep my eyes fixed upon where she was I felt towards her a sense of initiative which was perhaps after all one of the guises of love. Anna was something which had to be learned afresh. When does one ever know a human being? Perhaps only after one has realized the impossibility of knowledge and renounced the desire for it. (*UTN*, p. 238)

*

Murdoch's next book, *The Flight from the Enchanter*, appeared two years later, in 1956. It was received well, if with some reservations; its strengths and weaknesses, while noticed from the start, have become clearer in the light of later work. With its many internal echoes and its general busyness, the plot can seem too complex for the book's length; at the same time it states clearly a preoccupation with power relations – 'a particular kind of mythology that interests me is that of the power figure: the figure who is elected, as it were, to be God by other people, and made into a god who is a kind of false god'[14] – that would be a lasting concern. We may assume that the title's 'flight' is Rosa Keepe's, and that the 'enchanter' is Mischa Fox. Secret fantasy now plays a much bigger part, and this is particularly expressed through Murdoch's interest in the tendency of a group of people to bestow structure by allocating roles. Chief among these is that of the power figure, around whom other characters serve as demonic attendants. In this book in particular, many of these special roles are taken by 'foreigners' and almost by virtue of their foreignness (in this matter Murdoch becomes much more subtle later). These aspects of human behaviour are related to fundamental questions of form, opening up her work towards a certain kind of fantasy. In theory at least, this allows her as a novelist to conceive of her characters as individuals within a patterned whole without denying them each their aspect of freedom. And this problem gives particular cogency to her later quest for what she calls a 'peripheral' novel, one that is not overwhelmed by a 'magical pattern' and which is attentive to characters who cannot be regarded as at the centre of the plot or pattern. There are inherent paradoxes here, involving the relation between pattern and contingency, fantasy and the right to freedom of the free, full, rounded character, which have lasted as issues throughout her work.

Mischa Fox is indeed a sort of magical pattern maker, and the group's bestowal of importance on him is indicated, effectively if not very elaborately, by his different coloured eyes and his remarks on the ease of achieving fame for no very specific reason (*FFE*, p. 81). Several commentators have objected to him, on the grounds that his presence in the book is not weighty enough to do convincingly what is demanded of him; certainly later Murdoch power figures are more complexly present in their novels. Mystery here, however, indeed tends to be substituted for real action, easy assertions of power for its complexity. So Nina, the dressmaker, suffers unrequitedly from having elected Mischa to play the role of lover in her life, although this provides her with sufficient motivation to play a very small part in the interstices of his. Later she contemplates escape to Australia but – unlike Rosa Keepe – lacks the power to carry out her plans; her suicide is the first Murdochian death. Several alternative visions of power are more briefly indicated: John Rainborough imagines a state of affairs with his secretary Miss Casement very different from the reality offered to the reader; Annette Cockeyne fleetingly entertains the notion of making Nina a retainer in her own life (*FFE*, p. 75). Such moments contrast with Mischa Fox's exercise of the power which so many of the novel's characters so readily grant him. But *The Flight from the Enchanter* leaves us more with an impression of the universality of power rather than of its complexity.

The more complex story is that of Rosa Keepe, which, if not always fully realized, is far more interesting than those

33

mentioned. She exercises power over the demonic Lusiewicz brothers before the roles are reversed and she becomes enslaved by them, so to be captured on photographic film by Calvin Blick, Mischa's confidant, who in a 'technical excursion'[15] sadistically allows Rosa's brother Hunter to develop the exposure (*FFE*, pp. 159ff.). Apart from a past affair with Mischa, Rosa's other major relationship in the novel is with Peter Saward – the only character to refrain from electing Mischa to a position of power. (Murdoch has described him as a not altogether successful outsider figure who 'represents an open world'.[16]) He feels an attraction for Rosa which she declines to reciprocate, and for much of the novel's course she is struggling to free herself from Mischa. She is the character who is confronted with the consequence of her muddled actions, when Calvin Blick shows her the photographs (which force her to see herself in the Lusiewicz brothers' arms) and causes her to recognize culpability for her neglect of Nina.

Much of the interest in the book lies in its distinctive balancing of the strange and the realistic. At a fairly obvious level, the gods and demons who make their appearance here need not be inconsistent with realism, for they are 'there' in the novel in so far as they are seen to be created by the characters, not by the perverse imagination of the author – so that the author simply, so to speak, 'observes' them in action. This tactical relationship between author and characters is not unlike that found in other fictional contemporaries, like Muriel Spark and John Fowles, who have also balanced romantic forms against realism. But in Spark there is little of that compassionate moral dimension with which Murdoch invests the situation, and in Fowles the authorial ego is both imaginatively and technically far more pervasive. What is clear is that romantic and fantastic and Gothicized forms of fiction have played their part in a phase of the novel which has often been seen as pre-eminently realistic; this is one reason why Murdoch's use of this term needs careful analysis. With *The Flight from the Enchanter* we have a growing sense of the corporately magical nature of grouped human relationships, a sense of elusive but almost symbolic patterning which arouses our own allegorizing instincts and invests them in her characters, according to a clear mythopoeic impulse. In Murdoch's definition of art the coexistence of 'free' individuals with a sense of pattern as 'deep myth which comes, quite involuntarily, I think, out of the unconscious mind',[17] is of a very particular urgency.

And here we should not miss the significance of the dedication of *The Flight from the Enchanter* to Elias Canetti – evidence not only of Murdoch's long-standing and serious concern with modern European literature but of a certain kind of literary indebtedness which has grown more important. Canetti's influence on her seems at least two-fold. There is his general interest in the psychology of crowds and power – although his major work *Masse und Macht* (1960), which Murdoch reviewed in the *Spectator* when the English translation, *Crowds and Power*, appeared in 1962, post-dates this novel. There is also his own remarkable novel *Die Blendung* (1935; trans. 1946 as *Auto da Fé*), which can be seen as expressing just that kind of modern realism admired by Murdoch. If there are thematic tributes to Canetti in *The Flight from the Enchanter*, the most obvious would lie in the portrait of Peter Saward, the obsessive Babylonian scholar working on the Kastanic script, who seems indebted to Canetti's powerful profile of the brilliant bibliophile sinologist Peter Kien. Kien, whose personal tragedy comprises *Auto da Fé*, is a portrayal of a kind of accidental man, a figure of much concern to Murdoch. His relationship with books is central to his story; he values his books more than anything else, and marries his housekeeper Thérèse on discovering that her respect for them is even greater than his. When he speaks to her of the monetary rather than inherent value of the collection, he feels that he has betrayed himself; later, despite himself, money comes to dominate his marriage. Likewise, in Murdoch's early work the relation of money to power is frequently inspected, so that, for instance, the only way Rosa and her brother can save the *Artemis* magazine from a takeover by Mischa is to club with their elderly shareholders to buy it. By contrast, Saward, lacking in materialism, is also free of Mischa Fox. Canetti's novel opens out into the fantasy life of the human being, presenting it without authorial judgement. (Kien, threatened by Thérèse's encroachment into his study, loses his reason and joins up with his books to declare war.) With her second novel, Murdoch seemed to be stepping in a similar direction, drawing the book towards the obsessive, inward world of the characters' minds. Yet with *The Sandcastle*, her next novel, there seems another turning of direction.

*

The Sandcastle (1957) comes as perhaps more of a surprise the further away we are from it. It deals with the most ordinary and everyday environment in the Murdoch canon to date, being set among the staff of a Home Counties boarding school. Generically it seems familiar too: it is a love story, ending in renunciation. But, although it has been criticized for its decided thematic similarity to the conventional literature of women's magazines, it is more like its predecessor in its basic moral and narrative assumptions than is sometimes realized. A superficial account of its theme would concentrate on Bill Mor's attempt to escape an unfulfilling marriage by becoming involved with a young painter, Rain Carter, who has been commissioned to produce a portrait of the school's ex-headmaster, Demoyte. By the end of the book Mor, having been manipulated by his wife Nan, renounces not only Rain but the school as well, and embarks on a career in politics.

A bald summary such as this, however, fails to take into account the extent to which Rain Carter operates here much as Mischa Fox does in *The Flight from the Enchanter*. She, like him, is a central figure around whom others – not just Mor, but Demoyte as well, and possibly even Mor's jeweller friend Tim Burke – weave fantasies. The level at which these operate is less mysterious than in the earlier novel; the reader may well identify it as 'merely' sexual. But it must be admitted that here Murdoch's skill lies in conveying the extent to which Mor declines to show awareness of what is happening to him. His opening moves display his considerable reluctance to admit to the explicit consequences of his involvement with the girl, who in fact represents many different kinds of escape: to youth, wealth and a life away from the constriction of his marriage. (Mor and his family are short of money and painfully conscious of it.) Murdoch might well urge that we see Mor's career at the school as an example of the unexamined, yet by that token potentially virtuous, life; in this case the relationship with Rain would form another expression of the artist–saint contrast. However, one would be faced here with its expression in terms of the unconsoling truth that shortage of money can poison relationships and that, conversely, they can be imaginatively invigorated by money. All this would be to reckon without the figure of the 'anti-art artist',[18] the art master Bledyard, who alone remains not just resistant to, but apparently unaware of, the spurious fantasy charm exercised by Rain (S, pp. 210–14). Bledyard is apprehended as ludicrous in everyday life, but capable at heightened moments of rising to a certain gracefulness. Yet, even with his objectivity to guide us, we may be faced with an artistic failure in The Sandcastle resulting from the reader feeling too far outside the novel's values to be able usefully to identify with Mor. If so, Rain becomes no more than an affected little tease, for whom Mor acts, as they both admit to each other (S, p. 301), as a substitute for her recently deceased father.

Mor may be as deluded as Bradley Pearson, the narrator of The Black Prince (1973), and both men compulsively lie at critical moments, but somehow the relationship between Bradley and Julian Baffin is more palpable to the reader's imagination. Even though so much of the narrative of The Sandcastle uses Mor as an almost Jamesian centre of consciousness (the influence of Henry James, first discernible here, is to persist for some while in Murdoch's career), the sense of mystery surrounding the beloved object – that central Murdochian concern – becomes, I think, irritating with Rain, whereas Julian's mystery is somehow maintained. Why this should be so it is difficult to say, unless it is because Mor himself is too greyly realized a character to show convincingly the depth of fantasy attributed to him in the novel and on which so much of its effect depends. If this is so, the fault in this novel could presumably be identified as a technical one arising from an irreconcilable clash between the author's conception of Mor and the ways in which Mor's consciousness is allowed to reveal itself through the narrative. One instance can serve: on the afternoon of the mysteriously escapist car drive which will culminate in Rain's green Riley overturning into the river, she decides to swim. The powerful sexual potential of this scene does not seem to affect Mor sufficiently for us to be in turn interested in him. We may compare Mor's 'turn[ing] quickly away' at the sight of Rain's clothes lying on the river bank (*S*, p. 92) with Jake's articulation of his feelings on picking up Anna Quentin's shoes, or Bradley Pearson's interest in Julian's clothes and footwear. Murdoch has spoken of the secrecy of people and the power of the novelist to disclose fantasies such as would not be admitted even in psychoanalysis. The art in which she excels is precisely for this reason *not* the art of restraint with which we are confronted in *The Sandcastle*, but one of display – and of some exoticism – which is quite alien to the mode of portrayal chosen for Mor. While in many ways the quiet and everyday world offered in this novel is one which she believes the novelist should not consider unworthy of attention, it is a world to which her own fictional talents are simply not best suited.

Murdoch has recently remarked that she feels her chief failure in *The Sandcastle* was that of not having attended sufficiently to the specificity of Nan Mor. She now considers that Nan was in an almost Lawrentian way 'coerced':

it would have been a far better novel if I had spent more imaginative time detaching Nan from the story and not letting her just play the part of this rather tiresome wife but making her somebody with quite extraordinary ideas of her own, playing some quite different game, perhaps, having some dream life of her own which is quite different from that of the other characters.[19]

The interest of these remarks lies in the way they help to justify the role in the story of the Mors' daughter, Felicity, who lives a secret imaginative life undreamt of by her parents – as many younger Murdoch characters do. But here the feyness which worries so many of Murdoch's readers performs a realistic role in that it highlights the specificity of this character. Felicity's 'witchery' is fraudulent, so that while it is to be seen as precisely not bringing about the events desired, it does happen to coincide with them. Felicity's 'familiar' Angus never manifests himself in the shape of people she knows; the spectral dog Liffey is invisible to human eyes. Felicity adaptably interprets the portents which her activities provide. At a crucial point in the book, Angus takes on the form of a gipsy.

Critics of *The Sandcastle* have been disturbed by the gipsy and by his possible claims to being a 'symbol' in the book. It is often noticed that he leaves the scene at the end of the novel's action, having appeared at various sinister, resonant moments during it, notably on the afternoon of the ill-fated car ride. The way in which the gipsy seems to function is rather like the case of the bell in the next novel; both are accorded symbolic value by the characters in whose presence they operate. Murdoch's conception of symbolism is more scrupulous than is often maintained, precisely because she does not seem to see the symbol as something which only artists create. Rather, we as readers are all artists, or artists *manqués*; 'ordinary people' are symbol makers, and one consequence of realizing this is an understanding that symbolism usually comes in a Murdoch novel to operate in a subordinate and undominating way. It may illuminate character and this is perhaps to be thought of as its central role; an enchanting object or person may be given symbolic status by the (other) characters, but the way in which each character does this will be different, and the difference is a function of the characters' distinct existence as human beings. The process is more centrally and complexly evident in *The*

Bell, where the functions of 'symbol' and 'power centre' are strikingly linked; it would be quite wrong to think of the bell as operating in terms of the kind of dominant symbol which acts as a piece of currency with the same significance to all characters and readers.

None the less, there remains in many critical minds a sense of unease about the texture of the narrative of *The Sandcastle*, and a feeling that the everyday surface is seriously ruffled by dislocating elements such as the high level of dramatic adventure. Episodes here, in addition to the lengthy description of Mor's and Rain's attempts to get her car out of the river, would include the tower-climbing sequence involving Mor's son Donald and his friend Carde. Possibly the novel's greyly claustral milieu exacerbates the vivid nature of such episodes; certainly Murdoch persisted with the combination of adventure within a closed environment in *The Bell*, and here she may be felt to have been more successful in making the blend palatable.

*

The Bell continues, from the point of view of narrative, the mode deployed in *The Sandcastle*. Much of the action is apprehended through the consciousness of Dora Greenfield, who joins her husband Paul, an art historian, at a religious community, Imber, in Gloucestershire, where he is working on some manuscripts. What is new in *The Bell* is that Murdoch is at pains to fill out at some length the background of some of her characters, and the novel opens with an expository account of the circumstances leading up to Dora's rather unsuccessful marriage. This material is later complemented by a detailed account of the previous career of Michael Meade, one of the leaders of the community and the other major centre of consciousness. The development represented here is of considerable interest in the light of Murdoch's most recent work. A few serious readers at the time were prepared to come to terms with what she was attempting. In an important uncollected review in the *Spectator*, Frank Kermode pointed out that the 'dullness' of some of the expository prose could be seen to have 'an intelligible function', and noted some stylistic resemblances to E. M. Forster. Kermode went on to suggest that the characteristic Murdochian element of the improbable situation 'describ[ed] in validating detail' was being appropriated more closely than ever before to the demands of the narrative material itself.[20] Kermode pushed his argument further than merely claiming that the detail is 'relevant' to the plot; he suggested that the situation being described in the novel 'is given ... a quasi-allegorical significance which uses up the detail'. But as we have seen, full-blown allegory would run quite counter to many of Murdoch's theoretical views on the novel, and Kermode is duly careful with his formulation. The matter returns in a particularly interesting form in *A Fairly Honourable Defeat* (1970), of which Murdoch has herself offered an allegorical interpretation, while at the same time stressing that the novel must stand up without such interpretations.

The community in *The Bell* disintegrates after a while, unable to stand the various pressures on its existence. These culminate with the suicide of Nick Fawley, who had as a schoolboy of 14 terminated and confessed to a passionate homosexual relationship with Michael, who was then teaching at his school. Michael's hopes of the priesthood dashed, he had eventually devoted himself to setting up the community at Imber. After his betrayal of Michael, Nick had gradually drifted out of his life, returning to the community as an alcoholic in need of rehabilitation. Meanwhile Nick's twin sister Catherine had been preparing herself to enter the abbey at Imber as a nun. Prior to the events related in the novel, Paul had discovered during the course of his researches a legend concerning an old bell at Imber, and he tells Dora of this. The old bell reputedly lies in the lake in the grounds of Imber, having apparently flown out of the bell-tower after the discovery that one of the nuns had a lover; the nun subsequently drowned herself. Paul reveals, to Dora's annoyance, that the only other person to whom he has told the legend is Catherine.

The old bell is independently discovered by Toby Gashe, an 18-year-old boy in between school and Oxford, who is visiting Imber on a working holiday. Dora's estrangement from Paul leads her into Toby's company, the more easily as Toby is struggling to assert his heterosexuality after discovering that Michael is attracted to him. Together Toby and Dora decide to raise the bell in time to substitute it miraculously for the new bell, which is due to be installed in the abbey after a consecration ceremony. There is a farcical series of episodes at the ceremony, and an extensive description of the nocturnal attempts to raise the old bell. The substitution is effected, but not in the miraculous way Toby and Dora have planned. During the ceremony of installation the old bell falls off the causeway leading to the abbey and into the lake. As a rescue attempt is mounted, Catherine tries to drown herself. Unlike Ophelia, Catherine – attempting a tragic action – is rescued by an 'aquatic nun' (B, p. 284), the sight of whom, in her underclothing, is ludicrous, touching and taboo. Catherine, now deranged, is hospitalized.

A brief account of the plot will have served its purpose if it has shown something of the extent to which plot and pattern now emerge as matters of great interest to Murdoch. There are two main strands to the compulsive repetition of an action which has been damaging in the past. Catherine's behaviour may be thought of as a subconscious identification with the drowned nun, with whom Dora, though more robustly, also identifies on hearing the legend (B, p. 43). Catherine's identification and her spectacular renunciation of her vocation are presumably intensified by pressure from the rest of the community, coupled with her own repressed desire for Michael. It is not hard to appreciate the effect of such circumstances on a febrile personality. Michael is tormented by a recurrent and foreboding dream. In his waking life, submitting in an unguarded moment to his attraction for Toby, Michael kisses him and impulsively performs an action similar to that which had previously led to the destruction of his career. Nick, forcing Toby to 'confess' to the Olympian James Tayper Pace, repeats

42

his own act of betrayal and ensures that destruction. Michael quickly appreciates after Nick's suicide how perfect an act of revenge that final move has been, and he ultimately perceives himself as diminished by these events; Dora, on the contrary, emerges from them strengthened.

The repetition of an action from the past has informed the plots of previous novels; but in *The Bell* it assumes a new centrality and bestows apprehensible form on the entire narrative. It may be speculated that while this was pleasing to Murdoch on an aesthetic level, it was also giving her some cause for theoretical concern, and it is possible to detect certain tensions in the theoretical work which she was producing at this time. Accordingly, this chapter can usefully end with a brief indication of what this work contains.

*

In three essays, 'The Sublime and the Good' (1959), 'The Sublime and the Beautiful Revisited' (1959) and 'Against Dryness' (1961), Murdoch in effect offers a palimpsestic approach to a complex of problems lying on the edges of moral philosophy and literary criticism, although she has always stressed that she does not write as a critic. These issues constitute an enquiry into the nature of art, with particular emphasis on great literary art, relating it, in 'The Sublime and the Good', to morals and the making of moral judgements. Her enquiry involves her in taking issue with Kant's theory of the sublime, and by means of careful consideration of its inadequacies developing the notion that the common essence shared by art and morals is love, 'the extremely difficult realization that something other than oneself is real'.[21] It is therefore precisely the 'unutterable particularity' of nature and not (as we might be compelled to argue from Kant) its formlessness which should excite our *Achtung* (attention).[22] Our contemporary *malaise*, argues Murdoch in 'The Sublime and the Beautiful Revisited' and 'Against Dryness', lies in developments in the history of western European thought and expressed both in linguistic empiricism and existentialism, both of which make man, in effect, his own measure, and too readily push literary conceptions of man in the direction of either 'convention' or 'neurosis'. The former leads to a version of the literary hero she refers to as 'Ordinary Language Man' and the latter to 'Totalitarian Man'. Neither are in themselves adequate to express that sense of human nature which is found in the greatest literary art of Tolstoy or Shakespeare.

A. S. Byatt, one of Murdoch's most perceptive readers, attaches great importance to this theory. She argues that in *The Bell*, James Tayper Pace, in his inability to deal with Michael's predicament, offers an instance of Ordinary Language Man, and Michael, unable to deal with Nick, an instance of Totalitarian Man. But while *The Bell* thus has about it the sense of an imaginative critique of the theory, it is superior to it in patiently exploring the theoretical concepts for their applicability to real life. (In this sense Murdoch's practical presentation of homosexuality is profound.) As Byatt puts it, convention and neurosis are not used in the fiction as 'total patterning devices'; James and Michael are 'free' characters because in them Murdoch 'explores the fluctuations between vision, convention, neurosis and fantasy'.[23] It is clear, as Byatt argues, that there are many points of sympathetic contact here between Iris Murdoch's work and that of John Bayley. Both are aware of the extent to which convention and neurosis are capable of being used in fiction as instruments for the exploration of character and motive.

The situation which Iris Murdoch outlines in these essays is one which she sees as intensely problematic. She identifies and comments on two kinds of attempt to solve the problem which she sees as characterizing contemporary fiction:

> to solve it by denying freedom to the fictional individual either by making him merely part of his creator's mind, or by treating him as a conventional social unit, is likely to be a sort of failure. To speak of failure here has nothing disgraceful about it. Almost every work of art is a failure. The point is that this particular type of failure is one that we ought never to cease worrying about.[24]

Freedom here is seen to consist neither simply in a portrayal of man's solitary bravery in respect of an 'easily comprehended empirical world',[25] nor alternatively in a form of solipsism. It depends on a textured picture of man viewed against a background of transcendent reality, and presupposes a desire for the particular which is also a desire for the good. Hence, we may assume, the desirability of a careful, attentive portrayal of the natural world (something at which Murdoch in her most recent work comes to excel), and of the order of relationship which the individual has to it. The ills of convention and neurosis are best seen in the way in which they lead too easily into fallacies of form, to the production of work which, as she famously puts it, is either 'journalistic' or 'crystalline'.[26] But the attempt to resolve this itself quickly leads to the problem of discerning the right nature of form in art: 'Form is the temptation of love and its peril, whether in art or life: to round off a situation, to sum up a character. But the difference is that art has *got* to have form, whereas life need not.'[27]

Therefore, as she tells us in 'The Sublime and the Beautiful Revisited', 'to combine form with a respect for reality with all its odd contingent ways is the highest art of prose' (p. 271). We may take Murdoch's reflections on character and the need for indeterminacy, on the power of form and its dangerous consolations, on the practice of love and its place in the pursuit of goodness, her sense of fiction as a creative process of individuation, as illuminations of, rather than clear prescriptions for, her kind of fiction. None the less these issues express the dilemmas and the questions with which Murdoch continued to struggle in her novels of the 1960s.

3

'A SEVERED HEAD' TO 'THE TIME OF THE ANGELS'

The publication of *A Severed Head* in 1961 ushers in the period until 1966 in which a Murdoch novel appeared annually. This phase is the most problematic of her career; it alienated some of her early admirers and provided more fuel for her detractors than has any other. It brought her wide notice as a novelist of cerebral, sexually adventurous fiction, which could show an alarming tendency to turn into unconscious self-parody, and in which in their erotic behaviour the characters frequently over-step conventional barriers of age, gender and blood relationship. The field of action is largely restricted to a narrow band of the wealthy bourgeoisie, and a languorously decadent atmosphere is often characterized by richly described, decorative interiors, much heavy drinking, lachrymosity, suffering and fatigue. Darker themes sounded for the first time in *A Severed Head* include the beginnings of an interest in clothes which approaches the fetishistic, and abortion as a feature off-stage or in the past of certain characters. Perhaps the biggest problems have appeared in retrospect, as it has become increasingly evident that there is a serious divide between the most characteristic of these novels and the nineteenth-century models advocated in Murdoch's theoretical work dating from this period and later.

A Severed Head received a mixed press characterized by considerable puzzlement as to the direction Murdoch's work now appeared to be taking. There was some shrewd and interesting comment. Ronald Bryden, expanding on a noticed parallel with E. M. Forster, pointed out how Forster switched early in his career from the Italian comedies to the mode of *Howards End* (1910).[28] In an eccentric piece in which the oenophile may be discerned struggling with the literary critic, Cyril Connolly doubted whether a responsible wine merchant would risk his palate with as much whisky and gin as does Martin Lynch-Gibbon, and went on to distinguish usefully between the real sexual irresistibility of Palmer Anderson and Honor Klein, and the sham irresistibility Martin believes himself to possess.[29] This does at least draw attention to Martin's existence as a deluded narrator of the kind familiar from Henry James, and one whose cathartic experiences do not necessarily make him a wiser man, even though he seems at the novel's end to assert himself by matching Honor's power over him.

A Severed Head is narrated by the urbane, Anglo-Irish Martin Lynch-Gibbon, whose complacently successful marriage and concealed adulterous relationship are threatened and destroyed by the narrated events. These take the form of what Raymond Queneau referred to in his review of the book as 'matrimonial . . . *chassés-croisés*'.[30] There is indeed a symmetry that would have appealed to Henry James, the collector of *données* (though of course the material itself has an explicitness that James could not have countenanced); one is reminded of the 'Preface' (1907) to *What Maisie Knew* (1897) or the 'frame' to *The Turn of the Screw* (1898). The characters surrounding Martin, in a process which recurs frequently in Murdoch's fiction, begin to assert their independence in a way which affects not just Martin's present and future but also his view of the past. His wife Antonia falls in love with her American psychoanalyst Palmer Anderson, for whom Martin too confesses to a mildly obsessive interest. Later, Martin's mistress Georgie Hands becomes briefly engaged to his brother Alexander before attempting suicide, sending Martin her hair in place of the customary note, which Honor Klein receives. Martin himself, becoming 'fixated' with Honor, Palmer's half-sister, follows her to Cambridge to discover that she and

47

Palmer have been having an incestuous affair. But the greatest blow occurs towards the end as Martin is in a way dislodged from the centre of his own story. Antonia discloses that she has had a long-standing affair with Alexander. The symmetrical and potentially farcical aspects of all this may blind the less careful reader to some important 'work' which is going on here. In revealing what she does, Antonia effectively destroys Martin's valuation of the past, forcing him to realize that he exists on the periphery of other people's lives as well as in the centre of his own. The way in which Martin has interpreted every crisis so far must now be set against the interpretation forced on them by Antonia's revelation. For instance, Alexander's engagement to Georgie is now seen to have nothing to do with Martin; it is a gesture of pique on Alexander's part at having been replaced in Antonia's affections by Palmer. Of course Antonia's interpretation is not to be taken as 'true', any more than Martin's is, but it functions as a way of forcing him to attend to the 'otherness' of the surrounding cast in his narrated story. How much he has learned from this remains a matter of real doubt, since his very act of narration forces him to re-enact his past unawareness.

But if the way Martin is forced to reassess all his 'civilized' relationships points back to Jake Donaghue's reassessment in *Under the Net*, the dominant power relationships of the book are closer to those of *The Flight from the Enchanter*, but with new and strong Freudian overtones. The two power figures here are the anthropologist Honor Klein and the psychoanalyst Palmer Anderson, who, in their very incestuous relationship, become 'gods'. Honor in particular is granted prophetic powers, and challenges Martin to drop his 'talent for a gentler world' and enter one that had 'nothing to do with happiness' (*ASH*, p. 205). Through their role, a novel of bourgeois sexual relationships turns into a mythic tale with Freudian and Jungian overtones, as Martin is drawn towards Honor's 'dark gods'. In several interviews, Murdoch has spoken with affection of this novel, while admitting that the fact that it satisfies her own aesthetic taste more than some of her other

48

books should not necessarily lead us to think it better. Indeed, because there is so much of her direct, personal myth in it, a quest beyond society for the elusive character of reality, it may for that very reason be inferior. Like *The Italian Girl* (1964), which may in many ways be considered as a rather less successful treatment of the same kind of material, it was effectively dramatized: a testament at least to its clarity. Murdoch sees the character at the centre of the action in each play as 'a poor, rather gullible, confused man stumbling on from one awful blow to another';[31] perhaps in this sense her 'taste' should be seen in terms of that which first drew her to Beckett and Queneau.

A *Severed Head* is certainly a cunning comedy in a virtuoso manner, with ever extending sexual variation and a skilled use of repetition. Towards the end of the book Antonia, telling Martin of her affair with Alexander, pours most of her drink into his glass; to Martin the gesture seems 'vaguely reminiscent' (*ASH*, p. 186). The attentive reader remembers that the same gesture accompanied Antonia's telling Martin of her relationship with Palmer, early in the novel (*ASH*, p. 22). What is going on here? To Martin this seems a repetition; he is indeed 'stumbling on from one awful blow to another'. To Antonia it is quite different in kind; the second gesture accompanies a re-establishment of the status quo with Alexander, whereas the first marked a deviation from it. What looks like a repetition isn't, at least from Antonia's point of view. But it is Antonia who makes the gesture. Martin notices it but is unable to make the inference which his description allows the reader to make. At this complex level, actions which at first look like assertions are, when examined more closely, doing more than this. D. W. Harding complained of Iris Murdoch's work that frequently 'we are asked to accept explicit statements about feelings and motives instead of watching them arise intelligibly from characters acting within circumstances',[32] but the instance given surely provides one case where this is not so. In such ways Murdoch's narratives compel attention to detail: there is a comparable instance in *An Unofficial Rose* (1962) involving Mildred Finch dabbing citronella on Hugh Peronett, hoping by this sensory means to make him recall a kiss given twenty-five years earlier (*UR*, pp. 39, 68).

*

In *An Unofficial Rose*, a shifting to and from various centres of consciousness imparts an effect of authorial omniscience of which full and ironic use is made. From the point of view of narrative technique, it marks something of a return to the mode of *The Flight from the Enchanter*. *An Unofficial Rose* is a formally very beautiful work with a number of contingent graces which tend to mask the form, so that the reader's overall response is one of subdued, aesthetic pleasure at the blend. But several features have perplexed and irritated readers of this novel. The chain of unrequited affections, for instance, seems here, as implicitly in *A Severed Head*, almost wilfully self-parodic. The 'symbolic' potential of events and objects is now so strong as to make it hard for a reader to accept unreservedly the notion that such potential is bestowed by the characters alone: the novelist is evidently playing a part too. Perhaps this has been most strongly felt of Penn Graham's appropriation of the German dagger. In addition, a certain authorial intrusion seems to shape and guide some of the scenes in various chapters into ending in tableaux. The reader is left with a picture of Mildred Finch knocking over Miranda Peronett's dolls one by one (*UR*, p. 115) or of Randall Peronett kissing Nancy Bow-shott 'savagely' (*UR*, p. 185); this seems to be assertion without compensatory display, 'telling' without 'showing'. Possibly these features of the novel, and of several of its successors, are best seen in terms of an experimental holding in balance of necessity and contingency, which doesn't quite come off. But in *An Unofficial Rose* a certain stylistic 'staleness' may also be detected for the first time; in subsequent novels, certainly up to and including *The Time of the Angels* (1966), particular kinds of scene and, for instance, gesture are fallen back on rather, one suspects, because they have worked before in other contexts than because of any inherent appropriateness to the context in question. These features are still sufficiently slight, and redeeming characteristics sufficiently plentiful, for us to be able to think of *An Unofficial Rose* as a strong novel with some lapses. But after the rather different mode of *The Unicorn* (1963), Murdoch returns in *The Italian Girl* (1964) and *The Red and the Green* (1965) to what are arguably reworkings of former themes, while at the same time the grasp on stylistic freshness becomes less secure than ever.

An Unofficial Rose makes use of a more mannered form of the drama of a repeated action than we have yet seen, though the general pattern is familiar from *The Bell* and *A Severed Head*. Here the action is repeated not by the same character so much as representatively or vicariously in successive generations. This allows Murdoch to place great emphasis on the family; the 'court'-like element is noticeable both here and in *The Nice and the Good* (1968), a novel which has certain features in common with *An Unofficial Rose*. Actions and events are initiated and pushed around both by Mildred Finch from Seton Blaise and by Emma Sands from London. Both these characters visit the main court, Grayhallock, although Emma does so only once. Power so wielded is still completely a feature of the wealth of these characters; here as elsewhere the debt to Henry James is still strong (Murdoch admires James's ability to 'handle' money in his novels). In *The Nice and the Good* John Ducane's exercise of power is seen to be less dilettante and more closely related to obligations to society.

Recently widowed, Hugh Peronett, during the course of *An Unofficial Rose*, comes to contemplate his past in terms of failed potential: his one serious act of infidelity during his marriage was a brief but passionate affair with Emma. The momentary kiss with Mildred meant more to her than to Hugh. Hugh had drawn back from a relationship with Emma for a number of reasons connected with the security of his marriage. Emma, now a successful writer of detective stories, has as her amanuensis and companion in thrall the much younger Lindsay Rimmer, whom Emma at one point explicitly sees as playing Ariel to her Prospero (*UR*, p. 269). Hugh's son

Randall, wishing to learn more about Emma, has discovered Lindsay and fallen in love. The complex plot consists from this point of view of an innate comparison between the destinies of Hugh and Randall. Hugh's past choice, which he now admits to be the less fulfilling and potentially less happy one, is contrasted with Randall's choice making, which Hugh is forced to watch.

Randall leaves his wife Ann for Lindsay, having persuaded Hugh to sell his valuable Tintoretto painting and thereby provide him with the money for this adventure. Mildred, desiring a relationship with Hugh, finds herself – in a brilliantly comic scene of mistaken intentions – advising Hugh to take up with Emma again, a course of action which will release Lindsay for Randall. It later transpires that Emma has done just as much to initiate this release, having paid her one visit to Grayhallock not out of politeness but in order to decide to whom to leave her fortune. Ann, a mundane but therefore virtuous version of the truthful formless figure, is thereby made available to Mildred's brother Felix, Mildred realizing that both are inarticulately in love with each other. But for a variety of reasons, skilfully interlinked but themselves of varying degrees of convincingness, the vistas of freedom so allowed are not taken up. Among these reasons is Ann's truthful, non-fantasizing nature: she realizes the inadequacy of her love for Felix. Randall, having absconded to Italy with Lindsay, gradually finds the *frisson* of the affair evaporating. Miranda, the surviving child of Randall and Ann, has demonically desired Felix 'ever since she could remember' (*UR,* p. 254), and manipulates her mother into the destruction of the potential relationship with him. The turn of events is not unlike one's sense of confusions resolved at the end of one of Shakespeare's comedies, and Murdoch comes in more recent novels to make great use of Shakespearian comic form. As the novel ends, Randall seems about to repeat his father's action of returning to a second-best but securer relationship: Hugh is finally rejected by Emma and released for a promised journey to India with Mildred and Felix.

Human freedom is seen here in terms of the freedom to explore possibilities, although the way in which we actually react in the face of a freeing vista may be disappointingly cautious. The formal beauties of this novel suggest, as do others where the pattern is used, that the overall pattern of action is not apprehensible in equal measure to all the characters. Here, perhaps, the character with the greatest overall vision is Emma, the writer of detective stories. In first-person narrations which deal with the compulsively repeated action, the humour is blacker and more intense: the character is acting knowledgeably and in spite of himself. It is worth stressing that in *An Unofficial Rose* as elsewhere in Murdoch a comic sub-plot, organically related in an almost Shakespearian manner to the main action, reinforces the sense of pattern. The younger characters are seen to suffer as do their elders: this is another element which adumbrates *The Nice and the Good*. Penn and Miranda, cousins, each dimly apprehend the other's sexuality through what Murdoch has referred to in the Freudian terms of the operation of an 'egocentric system of quasi-mechanical energy . . . whose natural attachments are sexual, ambiguous, and hard for the subject to understand or control'.[33] The theme is most brilliantly and satisfyingly worked out much later in *The Black Prince*, but one can see in the relationship between Penn and Miranda the role played by, respectively, fetish and sado-masochism in adolescent fantasy. At an early stage Penn becomes fascinated by Miranda's knees; he is from then on 'in love' with Miranda in such a way that his feelings may be seen to be fantasy masquerading as love and brought on by his fetishistic apprehension. Miranda is sexually excited, towards the end of the novel, by the exercise of violence on Penn; she is interrupted by the sight of the German dagger (a present from Felix to her dead brother Steve) which Penn, having found, makes a pretext for visiting her. Later we discover (as, later still, does Ann) Miranda's secret collection of photographs, letters and press cuttings of Felix.

Possibly the emerging interest in Shakespearian form counters the interest in Jamesian style; at any rate Murdoch begins to detach herself from Henry James from this point on, sensing a dangerous seductiveness in James's rhetoric, while his centres of consciousness perhaps represent for her a threat to the desired blend of omniscient vision and novelistic display of states of mind. A quotation from *An Unofficial Rose* may serve to show the strength of James's influence at this stage in her career:

> Hugh leaned forward and took her chin in one hand and turned her face towards him. With his other hand he grasped her shoulder. The gesture had an effect of violence.
>
> She let him hold her so for a moment, and then shrugged him off. 'You see how much I need a chaperone!'
>
> 'So I'm to take Randall's place?'
>
> 'How prettily you put it. You're to take Randall's place.'
>
> He let out a long sigh and stood up. 'I wonder if I shall be able to stand it.'
>
> 'If you can stand it, come. And if not, not.'
>
> 'But you look so sad –'
>
> 'Ah, I'm not sad for now, my sweet, I'm sad for *then*.' (*UR*, p. 271)

*

The next two novels, *The Unicorn* and *The Italian Girl*, share a Gothic environment and certain other local characteristics, many of them rather negatively viewed even by Murdoch's sympathetic critics. It remains hard to see how much of the action in these novels, and in *The Red and the Green* and *The Time of the Angels*, can be credited even in terms of the fantasy-realistic fiction Murdoch claims to write. All four novels deal with peculiarly self-destructive families, and incest comes to be seen almost as a way of conveying internecine destructiveness and the raw nerve-endings of suffering. In *The Italian Girl*, David Levkin has made the narrator's niece Flora pregnant; after she has had an abortion, her mother Isabel reveals that he has also made her pregnant. There is a celebrated episode in *The Red and the Green* involving Millie

Kinnard and the sexual initiation of her nephew Andrew Chase-White in farcical circumstances in which three other men are involved.

In *The Unicorn*, Marian Taylor, recovering from an unhappy relationship, takes a job as governess at the remote Gaze Castle (presumably, though the country is never named, in Ireland). Once there, she discovers that she will have only one charge, not a child but the mistress of the house, Hannah Crean-Smith. From one of the few wholly articulate servants, Denis Nolan, Marian learns that Hannah has in fact been imprisoned in the house under the guardianship of her husband's ex-lover, Gerald Scottow, ever since she tried to murder her husband, Peter, seven years previously by pushing him over a cliff. She had, however, only managed to cripple him in some obscure and unrevealed way, and he had subsequently emigrated to New York. The *ménage* is completed by two poor relations: Jamesie Evercreech, who has been kept sexually and emotionally enslaved by Gerald every since he tried unsuccessfully to rescue Hannah, and Jamesie's older sister Violet, a somewhat sketched-in figure of doom. The nearest house is Riders, occupied by the Lejours: Max, the elderly, scholarly father, his son Pip and daughter Alice. Pip had been discovered making love to Hannah, and an ensuing struggle between Hannah and Peter had led to the murder attempt.

The title of *The Unicorn* draws attention, as does that of *The Bell*, to a central symbol whose attributes are not 'given' so much as bestowed upon it by the characters. Murdoch considers that the particular success of this novel lies in the way in which Hannah transcends the myth of the Christ-like suffering creature (Robert Scholes has pointed out that Crean-Smith is an anagram of 'Christ-name').[34] *The Unicorn* for Murdoch thus comprises a successful case of a character who 'eluded the pattern laid down by her creator', becoming 'involved in falsehood and guilt herself'.[35] This success must be offset by critical disquiet at the hectically melodramatic climax of the novel, with Gerald being shot by Hannah, Hannah drowning herself, and the crippled Peter, returning after the seven-year period is over, being driven through the floodwater by Denis and so (intentionally) drowned.

The central question in any assessment of *The Unicorn* must be how successful Murdoch has been in conveying the inner lives of her characters. The mode of narration is quite different from that of *The Bell* even though both are narrated in the third person. In *The Bell* there is no one central consciousness, and no easily discernible form or pattern to Murdoch's choice of narrative voice. In *The Unicorn*, however, there are only two consciousnesses, which are similar to each other and unlike any other character since they belong to the only 'outsiders' in the book, Marian and Effingham Cooper (a frequent guest at Riders). They have their own reasons, not consciously realized by themselves, for wishing to make the imaginative inferences which they do from the events they perceive. Their inability to be objective about what they are witnessing is rendered in various ways. One means which draws attention to it is the comic Murdochian device of the external world impinging by letter, frequently from correspondents who do not make any other appearance in the novels. Marian's correspondent is Geoffrey, whom she conclusively loses during the novel's course; Effingham's, Elizabeth, who remains available as the novel ends. Robert Scholes has a fine discussion of *The Unicorn* in which he shows that among the many levels on which it operates is that whereby Marian creates for herself a myth (the myth of the novel's title?) in which she decides 'to give a meaning of her own to her presence at Gaze'.[36] It is clear that, at this phase at least of Murdoch's career, it is this kind of psychological plausibility which constitutes the form of realism she is most interested in. The Gothic background may be seen in terms of that transcendent reality of which she speaks in 'Against Dryness'. The unlikeliness or bizarreness of many of the novel's episodes are subordinate to this transcendence, which places in perspective much of Effingham's egotistical reflection, including his pseudo-metaphysical insight when almost drowned in the bog.

The creation of myth by the characters within a given

narrative continues to occupy Murdoch in *The Italian Girl* and provides probably the most satisfactory way of approaching the ironic chapter headings (unique in Murdoch) of this novel. The narrator, Edmund Narraway, is another outsider, returning to his family home, where his brother Otto and sister-in-law Isabel have remained, for the funeral of their mother Lydia. Edmund plans to leave after the funeral but fails to do so. He is a man who sketches in his own past tantalizingly lightly but gives sufficient hints to indicate that he had left the family home out of unhappiness, has lived a monastic life as an engraver and, most puzzlingly, expresses surprise when asked by Maggie Magistretti, the Italian girl, whether he has ever been to Rome: 'It seemed odd she should not know. And yet why should she?' (*IG*, p. 115). The novel owes more than any other, as Elizabeth Dipple has shrewdly suggested, to the kind of thing Murdoch is happier doing when writing drama,[37] and there is almost universal agreement among Murdoch's critics that the dramatization of this novel, undertaken in collaboration with James Saunders, is more successful. In the novel as in James's *The Awkward Age* (1899), there is a high proportion of dialogue: Isabel, scarcely ever encountered outside the confines of her room, exclaims to Edmund: '"I'm caged, bored. I want emotion and pistol shots"' (*IG*, p. 36). The atmosphere of the novel has Russian elements and a striking affinity with the dramatic world of Chekhov.

The world of the novel's other characters is gradually revealed to Edmund, chiefly through sexual revelations involving the demon children David and Elsa, in ways which underline the emotional limitations both of Edmund himself and of these characters. He can seemingly only meet them one by one: the early chapters constitute in effect a series of disjointed interviews in which Edmund moves from one static encounter to another. There are many linking passages involving his running or chasing a character to the next encounter. This feature becomes less pronounced as Edmund becomes more involved with the character's world. His dry, crystalline fastidiousness cannot be kept apart from the wet, flabby, contingent

57

amorphousness of the world into which he is sucked; in this, his predicament is an extreme form of that of many Murdoch narrators, and ultimately a reflection of the artist–saint contrast. Edmund comes across as a ludicrously heavy-handed figure to whom everything must be explained; he is humiliated by Flora, his niece, whom he seems obscurely to desire. His only success lies in the attention he comes to give the Italian girl. This is the slightest of Murdoch's novels and was received the least favourably. In retrospect it now seems too skeletal to do justice to a talent best displayed in longer work.

The historical novel *The Red and the Green* followed in 1965. It is set in Dublin and environs in the week leading up to the abortive Easter Rising of 1916. There is no doubt that Murdoch researched her material carefully,[38] presumably in another kind of attempt to provide the desiderated transcendent background against which her characters could be seen to move. Many readers would agree that this background is portrayed with a serious effectiveness which the action itself undermines rather than enhances. It was possibly a mistake to use Millie Kinnard's escapade as a central episode, and it is tempting to suggest that if Murdoch were to rewrite the novel today she would have given more prominence to the character of the failed priest Barney, who is introduced when having fallen downstairs carrying some bottles of whiskey (*RG*, p. 51). At this stage in Murdoch's career, it must have seemed to many readers that her characters had simply been transferred from their more usual topographical environment to a historically authentic setting. Consideration of *The Red and the Green* raises the fascinating issue of the relationship between referential background and action in Murdoch's work although it may be felt that the combination of these two elements is not successful here.[39] A brief mention of a contemporary novel which does integrate historical Irish background more successfully with its action may be appropriate. The late J. G. Farrell's *Troubles* (1970) is set in the slightly later period of 1919–21; like much of Farrell's work it too was scrupulously researched. Farrell uses a decaying hotel, the Majestic, as his central location, and invests it with Gothic elements – owing something to the world of the cinema – which are not so much portentous (as in *The Unicorn*) as unfathomably comic. Against a surreal atmosphere the action is played out. Major Brendan Archer, returning from the Front in a condition similar to that of many survivors of the First World War, travels to the Majestic for the hand of his fiancée Angela, daughter of Edward Spencer. Although she dies shortly afterwards, having sickened with a mysterious complaint which turns out to have been leukaemia, Archer's connections with the Majestic are paradoxically strengthened, largely through his friendship with Edward, who becomes increasingly unbalanced in response to the Troubles. The entire narrative is invested with a wistful, ineffectual elegaicism; though the Major (always referred to as such) is the central consciousness, he remains far less accessible to the narrator than do the characters of *The Red and the Green*. The baffled omniscience characteristic of Farrell's narrator accords well in its restraint and its sense of accepted resignation with the background of a huge, crumbling and disintegrating edifice.

The Time of the Angels may be felt to conclude a rather unsatisfactory stage in Murdoch's career. Like many of her less successful novels, it is fascinating more for the thought that underlies it than for the working of that thought into the form of the novel's action and characterization. Carel Fisher, the priest who has come to believe in the death of God, in effect discovers that life in the full consequences of this belief is not to be borne. The intellectual debts are explicit: Nietzsche's *The Birth of Tragedy* (1872) and Heidegger's *Sein und Zeit* (1927) are pervasively present. Carel, appreciating that the statement 'There is no God' may itself have religious value, and attempting to come to terms with what lies behind the false, form-giving concept 'theology', invokes Nietzsche as one who 'for a little' understood what was at issue: '"Only his egoism of an artist soon obscured the truth. He could not hold it"' (*TA*, p. 171). Pattie O'Driscoll, Carel's half-Irish, half-black servant-mistress, reading a passage from *Sein und Zeit* on Carel's desk while cleaning his study, cannot comprehend it:

> The words sounded senseless and awful, like the distant boom of some big catastrophe. Was this what the world was like when people were intellectual and clever enough to see it in its reality? Was this, underneath everything that appeared, what it was really like? (*TA*, p. 152)

There are certain affinities between this novel and Murdoch's essay 'On "God" and "Good"' (1969), in which she investigates the possibility of a moral philosophy 'in a world without God'.[40]

Despite what may be felt to be its lack of success as a novel, *The Time of the Angels* does offer a form of the artist–saint contrast as a context for the exploration of its thought. The contrast is shown to have paradoxical workings: Carel is destroyed by what he believes; Marcus, his weaker brother, invigorated by intellectual and emotional contact with him. Carel is discovered by his daughter Muriel to have seduced Elizabeth, her cousin and joint ward of Carel and Marcus; later, Pattie tells Muriel that Elizabeth is in fact her half-sister. Carel is unable to survive Muriel's knowledge of this. Marcus, though himself agnostic, accepts the existence of form-giving theological myth; his humiliating encounter with Carel none the less compels him to abandon his never-to-be-completed work of 'milk and water theology' for a more truthful undertaking (*TA*, p. 196). An ironic sub-plot provides another perspective on the release of demonic energy in the relationships formed in the novel by the delinquent Leo Peshkov, whom *The Times Literary Supplement* reviewer considered as an unsuccessful version of Dostoevsky's anti-hero Verkhovensky.[41] Perhaps the most devastating view of this novel may be gained by appropriating remarks from A. S. Byatt's review of its successor, *The Nice and the Good*, to which the next chapter must turn:

> One of Iris Murdoch's great gifts as a realistic novelist . . . is a gift for analysing conscious thought in her characters as well

as unconscious impulses and emotional states. Her characters *think* and what they think and how (and how intensely they habitually think) affects what they do, which is what we find in life more often than in novels. In her more remote and Gothic novels her powerful central characters are largely symbolic, rigidly contained in a philosophical myth designed by the author. [*The Nice and the Good*] has no mythological centre and is the better for it. The ideas are worked out through the characters' reflections on them. . . . In a bad Murdoch novel [Radeechy] would have been important; here his small evil is placed by Ducane's vision of it as empty and puerile.[42]

4

'THE NICE AND THE GOOD' TO 'A WORD CHILD'

Division of any writer's work into 'phases' is, as will have been appreciated already, a notoriously arbitrary task. But it does increasingly begin to look as though in the novels which she published between 1968 and 1975 directions alter again, as Iris Murdoch came to see that one way out of the 'doldrums'[43] of the mid-1960s might be found in a more explicit reference to and use of Shakespearian comic form. *The Nice and the Good*, in atmosphere, treatment and subject matter, marks something of a break with its predecessors. Right from the urbane poise of the opening sentence the reader may sense a new, authoritative stylistic confidence. The quirks of previous novels ('X would survive', the 'gripping' of a table, repeatedly employed to accompany intense emotion, the over-reliance on the metaphor of the machine)[44] have vanished, and a descriptive capacity not really encountered since *The Bell* is now clearly in evidence. Here is the view from Trescombe House, the Dorset home of Octavian and Kate Gray:

> The front door was wide open, framing distant cuckoo calls, while beyond the weedy gravel drive, beyond the clipped descending lawn and the erect hedge of raspberry-and-creamy spiraea, rose up the sea, a silvery blue, too thin and transparent to be called metallic, a texture as of skin-deep silver paper, rising up and merging at some indeterminate point with the pallid glittering blue of the mid-summer sky. There was something of evening already in the powdery

goldenness of the sun and the ethereal thinness of the sea.
(*NG*, p. 19)

Passages such as these are complemented by a sense of amused,
ironic control over language, also largely absent since *The Bell*.
Occurrences of the word 'fungoid' in various contexts in *The
Nice and the Good* suggest a private joke surrounding the
relationship between omniscience and individuality, rather as
does a reference to the 'rebarbatively stony nature' of the beach
(*NG*, p. 58), which possibly reminds us of Toby Gashe's
fondness for 'rebarbative' in the earlier novel.

Octavian and Kate Gray preside over an extensive *ménage* at
Trescombe House, and the resemblance to the courtly world of
Shakespearian comedy in this novel is not hard to see.[45] The
household consists, in addition to Octavian's valetudinarian
brother Theo, of Mary Clothier (a widowed friend of Kate's
from university days) and Paula Biranne (divorced, and a more
recent addition). A younger generation comprises the Grays'
daughter Barbara, Mary's son Pierce (both in their teens) and
the formidably charming Biranne twins, 9-year-old Edward
and Henrietta. The group is completed by the housekeeper
Casie, Willy Kost (a refugee scholar who lives not in the house
but in a cottage on the estate), a dog (Mingo) and a cat
(Montrose). John Ducane, Octavian's colleague and friend, is a
frequent visitor.

Ducane is asked by Octavian to investigate the apparent
suicide of Joseph Radeechy, a minor and eccentric colleague
lower down the Whitehall hierarchy, in the hope that a scandal
may thereby be avoided. The novel's action alternates between
the London of Ducane's enterprise and Trescombe House. A
compromising story about Radeechy has already been leaked
to the press; Octavian is anxious to establish authoritatively
that no risk to security has been involved – and to do so without
the assistance of Scotland Yard. Ducane's enquiries lead him to
the conclusion that Radeechy's death was indeed a suicide, but
that it was committed not in solitude but in front of the man
who had previously alleged that he was the first on the scene

63

after the revolver shot. Like Radeechy, Richard Biranne is being blackmailed by Peter McGrath, the office messenger responsible for the press leak. McGrath had been assisting Radeechy in various ways in his black magic rites, eventually procuring his own wife Judy (who, as 'Helen of Troy', is integral to McGrath's blackmailing career). Biranne, a philanderer by nature, has been involved not only with Radeechy's wife Claudia but also with Judy. One evening, during a violent marital argument in his own home with Biranne present, Radeechy had unpremeditatedly pushed Claudia out of the window. Radeechy therefore carried out his final act in a spirit of revenge for what he felt to be Biranne's co-responsibility for Claudia's death.

From the point of view of his enquiry, Ducane is placed in a position of considerable power, since, as both men recognize, he holds Biranne's future career in his hands. To take the professionally correct course, an overwhelmingly attractive possibility for Ducane, and to round off his enquiry by demonstrating that Radeechy was not a security risk, Ducane would simply have to produce Radeechy's suicide note which Biranne had recovered but compulsively handed over to Ducane. Yet for a number of reasons Ducane is unwilling to exercise his power in such a way as to bring about the inevitable destruction of Biranne's career. In a deal which both men admit to be itself a form of blackmail, Ducane in effect agrees to present his report incomplete, in the sense that he will demonstrate the satisfactory closure of the Radeechy affair without bringing Biranne's name into it, provided that Biranne will agree to at least attempting a reconciliation with Paula. Ducane, professionally unsatisfied but morally at rest, offers his resignation to Octavian along with his report, ostensibly in order to be able to pursue his academic interests in Roman law on a more full-time basis.

In some interesting ways, Ducane's predicament and final decision can be seen as figurative of much that Iris Murdoch believes the novelist must do. Power and omniscience are dangerous weapons, and the artist must resist the too obvious temptation to round off a situation; though it should be said that having as it were drawn attention to this, Murdoch herself – characteristically effacingly – *does* round off this novel. She imposes formal pattern, having shown what contingency might involve; her contemplation of Shakespeare's comic form leads her to believe that he habitually does the same, though her own retreat from contingency in her novels seems also to be a statement of modesty. Ducane, elevated to godlike status by many of those with whom he comes into contact, largely because of his remarkable ability to elicit information and confidence, in many ways represents a realistic advance on earlier power figures. His predicament is complicated by a lack of clarity and decisiveness surrounding aspects of his personal life. He becomes appalled by his, in his own view, frivolous involvement with Jessica Bird and Kate Gray, and, like Biranne and Radeechy, is strongly attracted to Judy McGrath. He has to strive actively to detach himself from what these entanglements involve. Eventually, through the decisions he takes, the surrounding cast do come to perceive him as devoid of the mystique which they have bestowed upon him. And though he is 'independent' in the sense that he has inherited wealth, this feature is perhaps to be seen as a self-imposed challenge on Murdoch's part: she gets round potential problems surrounding wealth not by removing it but by making Ducane *work* differently from Mischa Fox or Emma Sands.

This complexity in respect of Ducane's predicament is orchestrated in the novel by means of some astonishingly dextrous patterning whose virtuosity for the first time in Murdoch performs really integral work. From the technical point of view, there is a new kind of narrative omniscience, so that while much of the action takes place through Ducane's consciousness, there are occasional 'distancing' reminders:

> Though Ducane did not fully realize it, his nervous uncertain sensuality needed some sophisticated intellectual encouragement. (*NG*, p. 26)

> though this was not entirely clear in his mind. (*NG*, p. 76)

Like most of her fellow students Jessica was, to an extent which even John Ducane did not fully appreciate, entirely outside Christianity. (*NG*, pp. 81–2)

These gestures towards omniscience are complicated by narrative jokes about the precise background and nationality of Fivey, Ducane's chauffeur. Ducane, Kate and finally Judy (who elopes with him), each believe Fivey to be a compatriot (respectively Scottish, Irish and Welsh-Australian).

In their turn, jokes such as these can be seen as forming a group of motifs which are complemented elsewhere, on a smaller or larger scale, by the twins' allusively intellectual games, the ludicrous epistolary approach and retreat from across the globe of Eric Sears, Paula's ex-lover, and Ducane's fleeting pensive references to 'girls and their dresses' (*NG*, pp. 274, 294). They exist, too, against a background of utterly horrifying contingent accident, such as that in which Mary Clothier's husband Alastair had been killed many years previously. And the patterns, whose details and wilfully intricate interconnections we may marvel at, play their part in revealing the confusions and deceits against which sexual relations are played out. In successive episodes, a naked Judy McGrath confronts Ducane with a whip; Ducane, discovering Pierce's sadistic hiding away of Montrose in order to gain Barbara's attention, confronts him with Barbara's riding-whip, and is in turn confronted by Mary, who is coaxed into telling Ducane (the first time she has told anyone) of the precise circumstances surrounding Alastair's death and her refusal to face up to it; Ducane successfully reaches Pierce after the defiant swim into Gunnar's cave and both, warmed by Mingo who has followed Pierce in, miraculously survive; Ducane and Mary fall in love. Juxtaposed with this complex of episodes reflecting the impure mixture of sexual motivation is the scene in which the reconciliation between Paula and Richard is played out in front of the Bronzino in the National Gallery (this detail may contain an echo from James's *The Wings of the Dove* (1902)). In a realistic and completely acceptable way, we are shown the truth of Octavian's remark that 'sex comes to most of us with a twist' (*NG*, p. 36), a remark made in the context of Radeechy but revealed as true of everyone in a manner which duly 'places' Radeechy.

*

Bruno's Dream (1969), framed in its first and last chapters by the dying consciousness of a very old man, has a plot which is initiated by a desire for reconciliation. Bruno Greensleave has failed in life, professionally (as an arachnologist), personally (as a husband) and in combination (as a stamp-collector), and alienated his son Miles long previously when faced with the prospect of an Indian daughter-in-law, Parvati. Shortly after her marriage to Miles, Parvati had been killed in an air crash, and Miles had responded to her death by writing a long poem before eventually remarrying. The relationship with Miles is capable of resuscitation; but Bruno remains tormented by the mess in which his own marriage had ended, with the discovery by his wife Janie of his affair with Maureen and Janie's subsequent death from cancer, while still unreconciled to him. The Greensleave printing works have been taken over by Bruno's son-in-law Danby, a widower now sleeping with the maid, Adelaide de Crecy; Adelaide in turn is a cousin of the Boase twins, Will and Nigel, formerly actors, though the mystic Nigel is now Bruno's nurse.

Bruno and Miles are in fact linked by the problematic nature of the relationship between death and consolation, and this is a relationship which has exercised Murdoch theoretically:

> It is the role of tragedy, and also of comedy, and of painting to show us suffering without a thrill and death without a consolation. . . . The great deaths of literature are few, but they show us with an exemplary clarity the way in which art invigorates us by a juxtaposition, almost an identification, of pointlessness and value.[46]

Thus while the extended treatment of Bruno's departing consciousness recalls Beckett, as A. S. Byatt pointed out in her review of this novel,[47] it is Murdoch's contemplation of Shakespeare's treatment of Cordelia, and her belief in the sublimity of *King Lear*, that are never far from the back of our minds here. From this point of view Frank Kermode articulated what is perhaps the central question: 'Does the novel make death poetic, as Miles's early, bad, poem did? [*Bruno's Dream*] examines itself on this.'[48] But the sublimity so suggested is challenged in this novel by what Lorna Sage has called Murdoch's 'aesthetic of imperfection'.[49] Potentially disabling elements, discernible in *The Nice and the Good* but veiled by the comic graces of that novel, are here left more barely exposed in an almost assertive manner. The tendency towards narrative dismissal of the characters, evident in the last chapters of *The Nice and the Good*, is distilled in the outrageous 'future history' of Will Boase and Adelaide de Crecy on their marriage. Little is conceded in the case of Nigel's crazy mysticism, even though his insights anticipate visions more challenging to Murdoch readers, such as Tallis Browne's demonic presences in *A Fairly Honourable Defeat*, and Anne Cavidge's encounter with Jesus Christ in *Nuns and Soldiers* (a novel, incidentally, also much concerned with non-consolatory death). To Lisa, Miles's sister-in-law, with whom both Miles and Danby have fallen in love, Nigel reveals himself: 'Maybe this is how God appears now in the world, a little unregarded crazy person whom everyone pushes aside and knocks down and steps upon' (*BD*, p. 210). Lisa herself, in love with Miles, elects to save his marriage to Diana and turns her attention to Danby, thereby admitting the conquest of muddled sexual motivation in her life, and surely recalling Murdoch's own related apprehension of sado-masochism in terms of 'plausible imitations of what is good'.[50] A further area of potential though self-imposed disadvantage may lie in the very use of the flashback mode, which presents Bruno's arachnological and philatelic interests as thin, concessive tokens not integrally characterizing him in the way that Ducane's interest in Roman law may be said actually to illuminate the latter's personality:

The immense literature about Roman law has been produced by excogitation from a relatively small amount of evidence, of which a substantial part is suspect because of interpolations. Ducane had often wondered whether his passion for the subject were not a kind of perversion. (*NG*, p. 166)

*

Iris Murdoch returns, in *A Fairly Honourable Defeat* (1970), to a novelistic mode similar to that of *The Nice and the Good*, both in its relative 'openness' and in its use of an enchanter figure. In *A Fairly Honourable Defeat*, as in its successor, *An Accidental Man* (1971), many potentially disabling elements are turned to explicitly comic use, and from here on in Murdoch's development it is possible to see this comic sense as attaining increasingly sophisticated solipsistic dimensions which reflect on the difficulties of handling the contingent mess of life within the constraints of the novel as a form. The 'purest' examination of the issues may be found in *The Black Prince* (1973). *A Fairly Honourable Defeat* and *An Accidental Man* are longer novels than any of their predecessors, and their nature is usefully characterized in terms of the ways in which both can be shown to adhere broadly to the pattern of Shakespearian comedy. In addition there are repeated specific allusions in *A Fairly Honourable Defeat* to *A Midsummer Night's Dream*, though the march of the plot seems to have more in common with *Much Ado About Nothing*. While Murdoch is continuously contemplating the non-consoling sublimity of *King Lear*, she seems also to be reflecting in these novels on her claim in *The Sovereignty of Good*: 'Perhaps one of the greatest achievements of all is to join [the] sense of absolute mortality not to the tragic but to the comic.'[51] In this ostensibly paradoxical sense, comedy may be the higher form.

The enchanter figure of *A Fairly Honourable Defeat*, Julius King, is arguably less successful than Ducane in that his character and function are not so satisfyingly integrated. But his actions, however dilettante, reveal an attitude to form as opposed to contingency which is a familiar one. Julius's tidying of Tallis Browne's unspeakably squalid flat reflects, as he himself admits, 'a passion for cleanliness and order' (*FHD*, p. 426), but this also entails disrespect for the contingent. Tallis's flat returns to its former state of malevolent disorder animated by scuttling beings at the end of the novel. Tallis cannot tidy up, yet can live with, his relationships with his (ex-)wife Morgan (also ex-lover of Julius) and his invalid father Leonard. Julius, who has been able to sever completely his attachment to Morgan, advocates telling Leonard the truth about the older man's cancer: as the novel ends, Tallis is resolving to do this. Julius's inability to deal with the contingent aspects of human relationships causes him psychosomatic ailments such as migraine and a complex of digestive disorders which heal up when he is on his own, as in the final chapter. In this, he is utterly opposed to Tallis: the relationship is a particularly clear statement of the artist–saint contrast, but in addition Murdoch has pointed to an allegorical dimension in which the diabolic Julius opposes the Dostoevskyan, Christ-like Tallis (at one point Julius asks Rupert whether Tallis is an epileptic (*FHD*, p. 221)). In such a schema, Leonard, for whom 'it all went wrong from the start' (*FHD*, passim), would be God the Father.[52] It is hard to ascertain how seriously Murdoch is advocating such a reading.

Julius succeeds in destroying the relationship between Rupert and Hilda Foster, though the destruction is partly accidental, as is Rupert's death. The homosexual relationship between Simon Foster and Axel Nilsson, endangered though it is by society, is ultimately strong and stable enough to withstand Julius's attentions. In her earlier essay 'The Moral Decision about Homosexuality' (1964), Iris Murdoch had conceded that 'the only serious and important part of the "hostile case"' was 'that a homosexual ménage is essentially unstable'.[53] This concession is not a judgement, and in the case of Simon and Axel the instability is admitted, examined and portrayed with sensitive respect for their individuality.

*

Murdoch's interest in the role contingency in general and accident in particular can and should play in the novel is shown in its most extensive manner to date in *An Accidental Man*. The central episode, in terms of its place in the novel, is Austin Gibson Grey's running over of a little girl while at the wheel of his brother Matthew's car and slightly drunk. He escapes prosecution but is blackmailed by the girl's stepfather (an aspirant novelist) until a mixture of physical assault on Austin's part and further accident reduces the blackmailer, Norman Monkley, to a state of mental vegetation. Concise plot summary is difficult in view of the enormous cast, but it would be true to say that much of the rest of the novel shows this accident in particular, as well as accident in general, reflected in facets of the lives of others. The action is interspersed with letters and characteristically 'stichomythic' conversations[54] involving other members of the cast, some of whom have no existence outside these sections of the book. Formal division into chapters is dispensed with in what has in effect become something of an established precedent. In addition to accident we are presented with failure to intervene, as with Austin's son Garth and a street murder witnessed in the United States, or Matthew and a political demonstration witnessed in Red Square. It is tempting to see these episodes as figurative of meditations on the novelist's role in the actions in the narrative. The plot makes great use of internal echo and motif: one particularly characteristic cluster, recalled by Dorina Gibson Grey just before her death, is the phrase '*C'est impossible de trop plier les genoux, impossible, impossible*' (*AM*, p. 105), which, finally identified as the words not of a holy man but of a ski-instructor at Davos, becomes 'another senseless fragment of ownerless memory drifting about like a dead leaf' (*AM*, p. 368).

Towards the end of the novel it is revealed that one of the characters existing only in the letter-writing sequences, a delinquent little girl named Henrietta Sayce, has fallen to her death from some scaffolding. This seems to illustrate an interesting paradox about death and suffering in their artistic portrayal, which is that certain kinds of repetition may rob accident of its claims to solitary, dignified tragic expression, and turn it instead into something which approaches comedy. The claim of the accidental death of a little girl to be considered 'tragic' is commented on by the repetition. It may be argued that the same sort of assault on solitary dignity is enacted in *King Lear*, where Lear's claims for the status of his experience are, as it were, undermined by the Gloucester sub-plot. The lesson learnt would have to do with the inescapability of form in human experience: form may be thought of as taking over, organizing and reminding us that artistic portrayal of the human predicament is likely ultimately to be not solitary but collective, not tragic but comic. Iris Murdoch herself has written lucidly of the death of King Lear:

> all good art is its own intimate critic, celebrating in simple and truthful utterance the broken nature of its formal complexity. All good tragedy is anti-tragedy. . . . Lear wants to enact the false tragic, the solemn, the complete. Shakespeare forces him to enact the true tragic, the absurd, the incomplete.[55]

Like *A Fairly Honourable Defeat*, *An Accidental Man* also treats – in terms of an individual case – a moral issue which has concerned Murdoch outside her fiction. Vietnam is not mentioned in the novel, but it may be assumed that Ludwig Leferrier's predicament is meant to reflect the moral complexity characterizing individual attitudes towards what Murdoch described in 1967 as 'one of the more wantonly wicked political actions of the human race'.[56] Ludwig's choice is between return to the United States, punishment for draft evasion and the inevitable destruction of a promising academic career, or residence in Britain (to which he is entitled by an accident of birth), with the settled life of an Oxford fellowship and a financially and socially secure marriage to a girl, Gracie Tisbourne, who is completely in love with him. What makes the choice agonizing is that this latter option is inextricably linked to Ludwig's knowledge that it may ultimately be no more than an abnegation of duty based on a false application of the parable of the talents, and Murdoch accordingly attends scrupulously to his character, temperament and cultural-religious background.

*

It is appropriate at this point to mention the two plays in Murdoch's small but distinguished dramatic output which are not based on any of the novels. *The Servants and the Snow* and *The Three Arrows*, first performed in 1970 and 1972 respectively, have something in common with the last-mentioned aspect of *An Accidental Man* in that both present highly complex moral dilemmas. They do so, however, in situations which are quite unlike anything in the novels. There is a claustrophobic remoteness about the two settings which allows these dilemmas to be presented in a particularly pure form. Each play in effect offers a dramatized debate on the nature of political power, and the form of the play results in attention being concentrated on the rhetoric of that power rather than, as in a Murdoch novel, on what she has referred to as the struggle being waged between form and character.[57] *The Servants and the Snow* presents a conflict between liberalism and tyranny set in the context of a feudal estate (possibly Balkan, though the peasants speak with Irish accents). The time is impossible to determine. The servants are perplexed by the liberalizing and reforming policies of the new heir, Basil, who succeeds an era of terror. Basil becomes increasingly ineffective, the surrounding situation deteriorates, and after his murder the state of affairs is efficiently, though ruthlessly, being resolved by his brother-in-law 'the General' as the play ends.[58] *The Three Arrows*, politically more sophisticated, is set in medieval Japan in the context of a power struggle between the effete imperial court (manipulated not by the Emperor but by his far more dynamic predecessor and uncle, Tokuzan) and the warrior aristocracy under the leadership of the Shogun, who really rules the country. Caught in a stalemate between the two is the political prisoner Prince Yorimitsu. Attempts are

73

made to resolve matters by appeals to Yorimitsu to enter the religious life of a Buddhist monastery, but these are not successful. A final assault on the stalemate comes about in a pair of comically juxtaposed scenes in which the Emperor's sister Keiko smuggles herself into Yorimitsu's presence (whereupon they fall in love with each other), and Tokuzan simultaneously decides to resolve the deadlock by having the couple betrothed and initiating the customary ordeal of the three arrows. Yorimitsu's success will entail instant marriage, and his failure instant ritual suicide: manipulating the result will tidy Yorimitsu out of the way without provoking the threatened civil war both sides have hitherto feared. Yorimitsu fails the ordeal but just as he is about to disembowel himself the Emperor intervenes; Keiko has, however, already stabbed herself. Yorimitsu escapes in the ensuing confusion and resolves, as the play ends, to enter the monastery after all.

*

From *The Black Prince* (1973) until the most recent novel, *The Philosopher's Pupil* (1983), the tendency towards oscillation between extremes, which Murdoch and others have long since noted in her work, became pronounced. Every other novel is a first-person male narrative, though the most recent narrator, N, is, as he puts it, 'discreet and self-effacing' (*PP*, p. 16). Interspersed with these first-person narrations are third-person narratives whose titles take the form 'X and Y' and seem to be presenting a dichotomy whose nature may be thought of as not unfamiliar yet whose terms are constantly being restated. The critical reception of these 'X and Y' novels has on the whole been rather less favourable than that of the first-person narrations, and it does seem to be the case that the first-person narration suits not just Murdoch's technical gifts but the presentation of her theme in novel form. The remaining discussion may show to what extent this view is justified.

The Black Prince is considered by many of her readers as her finest work. Certainly it is virtuoso in its technical self-consciousness; in the way in which it challenges its own text and reliability, and speculates on fictionality, it may be thought of as Murdoch's closest approach to the 'post-modernist' novel. Thematically, it represents a remarkably brilliant self-imposed challenge, since it is undoubtedly the most solipsistic of her novels: her theme, however, has constantly involved attention to the dangers of solipsism. In this respect it is in its way as dangerous an achievement on her part as her narrator, Bradley Pearson, argues *Hamlet* to be on Shakespeare's: '*Hamlet* is a wild act of audacity, a self-purging, a complete self-castigation in the presence of the god' (*BP*, p. 200). Shakespeare, sailing 'nearer to the wind' than in any of his other achievements, nevertheless escapes punishment. The traditional representation of divine punishment for artistic hubris has, since classical antiquity, been the flaying of Marsyas by Apollo (Ovid, *Metamorphoses*, VI). Given the name of the narrative's editor, P. Loxias, fellow-prisoner to Pearson, there can be no doubt that this myth underlies *The Black Prince*, and Loxias is referred to in Rachel's postscript as: 'a notorious rapist and murderer, a well-known musical virtuoso, whose murder, by a peculiarly horrible method, of a successful fellow-musician made the headlines some considerable time ago' (*BP*, p. 407). If in a mythic respect Loxias plays Apollo to Pearson's Marsyas, there is also a 'sensational' aspect to Pearson's narrative in which Pearson himself plays Apollo to the Marsyas of his rival Arnold Baffin, for whose murder he is imprisoned. There is no shortage of motive: Baffin is younger and more 'successful', and Pearson was in love with his wife Rachel before falling catastrophically in love with their 20-year-old daughter Julian; Arnold intervenes and wrests Julian away from Pearson.

It is not hard to see in Pearson and Baffin a particularly pure statement of the artist–saint contrast: Baffin's productivity is countered by Pearson's 'writer's block'. The work of art which his encounter with the god finally enables him to produce is capable of being described by at least one of its readers as 'a

75

piece of fantastic writing' (*BP*, p. 402). It has also been pointed out that the descriptions of Baffin's reputation and even of his work are a parody of unflattering views of Murdoch herself.[59] Baffin wrote 'too much, too fast' (*BP*, p. 51), and in a description which appeals to Pearson's (rarely evident) sense of humour, Julian says that Baffin 'lives in a sort of rosy haze with Jesus and Mary and Buddha and Shiva and the Fisher King all chasing round and round dressed up as people in Chelsea' (*BP*, p. 137). Yet it is hard to imagine that, in the view of *Hamlet* which Pearson advances to Julian, Murdoch's own thought is not present.

However, the view that Baffin and Pearson in their inter-action solipsistically represent warring elements in Murdoch's own artistic consciousness is rendered highly complex by the sense of unreliability that undercuts every element in the story. The most obvious manifestations of this are the editorial and narrative format and the device of the postscripts from four of the novel's characters, as well as the death of Pearson which renders counter-claim impossible. The editor points out what is all too obvious: every one of the four postscript-writers attempts to show that Pearson was in love with them. One, Francis Marloe, also points out something which, if it were not for the fact that Marloe points it out, the casual reader might be inclined to give more serious credence to: Pearson may be in love with Baffin.

In addition to the elements pointed out by Marloe, Pearson's own narrative is seriously complicated by his fetishism. One very central motif here is the pair of boots which Pearson buys Julian and which she wears to the *Hamlet* tutorial. At one stage during the tutorial the room becomes unbearably hot; Pearson refuses to open the window but allows Julian to take off her boots. After Pearson has discoursed on the play Julian reveals that she had once played Hamlet at school, when aged 16: '"I wasn't very good. I say, Bradley, do my feet smell?" "Yes, but it's charming"' (*BP*, p. 200). Having sent Julian away and revealed that he has fallen in love with her, Pearson, anxious to stress that what he is undergoing is not 'mere "sex"' (*BP*,

p. 205), characterizes his state of mind by saying that: 'Love generates, or rather reveals something which may be called *absolute charm*' (*BP*, p. 206). Yet the reader has already been invited to make the connection between boots, legs and sexual arousal in the shoe shop, and the word 'charm' seems morally suspect in Pearson's narrative. The smells which Pearson finds 'charming' in Julian nauseate him coming from Priscilla or even Rachel. Later, on their 'honeymoon', Pearson falls asleep in shirt and socks, 'a most unattractive *déshabillé*' (*BP*, p. 313), and is disconcerted on waking to think how he must have appeared to Julian. In the context of the fetishistic motif her reply, 'I love your socks', takes on great complexity.

It is in this general context that we must see Pearson's near-rape of Julian, after some unsuccessful love-making, once she has, for a joke, dressed up as Hamlet. This occurs, furthermore, once Marloe has contacted Pearson at the remote Patara to say that Priscilla has committed suicide. The death of his sister is clearly liberating for Pearson, Apollo and the dark god Eros are identified with each other, and the extent to which *Hamlet* plays its part is not altogether easy to establish. Here, in addition, there is reference to the tradition of sexual equivocation and disguise on which Shakespeare draws in his comedies and which the Austrian playwright Hugo von Hofmannsthal deploys in his elegiacally sensuous libretto to Strauss's *Der Rosenkavalier*, to which Julian has previously taken Pearson. Pearson has been unable to endure more than the first few minutes before having to escape into the street in order to vomit.

Fantasy and reality coexist in a complex, intertwined relationship in *The Black Prince*: a reader may well sympathize with the dignity of Pearson's experience while at the same time considering him deluded. His behaviour towards Julian, particularly, is seen to illustrate much that Murdoch has advanced theoretically concerning the role of sado-masochistic fantasy in life and art, though it also reminds us of what is less sympathetically remarked by Julius King: 'Human beings are essentially finders of substitutes' (*FHD*, p. 233). In her own way,

Murdoch also juggles with dangerous material here: sex is presented as coming to Pearson very much 'with a twist', yet the redeeming grace, present here and largely absent in the novels of the mid-1960s, is that Pearson's character, attentively explored, makes sense of the theory.

*

Further interaction between fantasy and reality is evident in *The Sacred and Profane Love Machine* (1974), a novel which treats in a buoyant and almost frivolous manner themes elsewhere handled more seriously, and elements of whose plot recall that of *An Unofficial Rose*. Blaise Gavender, a phoney psychiatrist, is forced to reveal to his wife Harriet and son David the nine-year existence of a second ménage with his mistress Emily McHugh when his and Emily's son Luca discovers the existence of the legitimate Gavender household. Though the moral issues here are attended to with characteristic seriousness, the aesthetic working out of the plot is much concerned with the demonic power which dreams and fantasies may exert on 'real' action, and the ways in which violent images may spill over into it. A central playfulness here surrounds the character of the Gavenders' recently bereaved neighbour, the detective writer Monty Small. It is symbolized by Monty's creation of Magnus Bowles, a supposed psychotic patient who is Blaise's alibi for the once-a-week evenings and nights spent with Emily. Monty's decision to kill off Magnus once it becomes clear that Harriet, in extreme crisis, proposes to consult Magnus about Blaise, brings about Harriet's flight to her military brother in Germany; her accidental death is an uncanny fulfilment of an agonized wish earlier expressed by Emily in her frustration at having to live an unacknowledged and futile life as Blaise's mistress: 'God, sometimes I feel like people who go to an airport with a machine gun and just shoot everyone within sight. You simply have no idea how much I suffer' (*SPLM*, p. 94). In a sense Harriet is tidied away, though not through the causal agency of Emily, and Blaise is free to remarry. To David, though he does not himself admit the reference, his father's 'obscene hasty marriage' (*SPLM*, p. 348) must make his predicament look very like Hamlet's. Further interaction between real and fantasy worlds is provided by the way in which the novel's single cited episode from one of Monty's 'Milo Fane' thrillers anticipates the episode in which Blaise is attacked by the Gavenders' starving dogs. Both episodes involve the severing of an Achilles tendon.

The sense of demonic forces at work is heightened by parallels such as these, with their aura of indiscriminate accident and punishment partly related to or brought about by imaginative fantasy, but Monty and Emily are not the only agents. A drunken intervention by Edgar Demarnay, who offends Monty's detached fastidiousness, prompts the final break between Blaise and Harriet. And the almost delinquent Kiki St Loy and Constance Pinn offer sexual solace at critical moments. On a smaller but not negligible scale, fantasy and reality are interwoven in the experiences of Blaise's patients, none of whom is as blatantly 'invented' as Magnus Bowles, yet none of whom is introduced into the novel's action except in the most fleeting way. One patient, Septimus Leech, previously in *The Black Prince* invented by Julian as a pretext for irritating Pearson and inviting him to *Der Rosenkavalier*, exemplifies one of a number of jokes applying to the Murdochian world and a sense too, it may be argued, of the confident good health of the contemporary novel. Here Septimus Leech is a blocked writer; in conversation with Blaise's other patients towards the end of the book, he shares an almost universal sense of jubilation with them and reveals that he has nearly completed his novel. But in a parenthetic throwaway which aptly exerts a dynamic effect on the preceding narrative, we are told: 'Only poor Jeannie Batwood was silent. She was desperately in love with Blaise and could not now leave him, even though her husband was threatening divorce proceedings' (*SPLM*, pp. 340–1).

At first glance *A Word Child* seems to raise familiar themes in familiar ways, but a closer look reveals some differences and developments from its predecessors. It should be stressed that in this novel, too, there is a relationship to material which has been aired by Murdoch in a non-literary, polemic context. In 1975, the year of publication of *A Word Child*, Murdoch contributed to one of a series of *Black Papers* arguing against government education policy in Britain, in so far as it seemed to favour the indiscriminate introduction of non-selective, un-streamed comprehensivization. At the end of this essay she urges that there is room for complacency in the face of such a state of affairs only as far as able, middle-class children 'with moderately bookish homes and educationally ambitious parents behind them' are concerned; she is manifestly worried about the fate of 'the poor clever children with an illiterate background who on the "chance" system are being denied the *right* to a strict academic education which can only be achieved on the basis of some sort of selection'.[60] The narrator of *A Word Child* comes from this latter background; Murdoch characteristically shows how strong even under the 'old' system the element of chance is, and at one level the narrative can be seen as examining or even challenging some of the theoretical assumptions of the *Black Paper* essay.

Hilary, a prostitute's child from an illiterate and almost utterly loveless background, has been 'rescued' because of the discovery of his linguistic aptitude by the schoolmaster Mr Osmand, a version – as practically always in Murdoch – of the good man. Hilary proceeded to pursue his study at Oxford with considerable success. While there he encountered and was befriended by Gunnar and Anne Jopling, who had also shown unwonted kindness to his half-sister Crystal, with whom Hilary describes himself as 'oned in love' (*WC*, p. 14). Mr Osmand appears only once in the novel, apparently *in extremis*, but it is entirely characteristic of Hilary's peculiarly appalling form of willed accident-proneness that he is unfit to help Osmand on this occasion, having (unaccustomedly) 'tripped out' through the hospitality of his flatmate, the ex-pop-star Christopher. Osmand is later discovered to have committed suicide, as we learn through a letter from his landlady. It is worth pausing to note again the decorative level at which

Murdoch is capable of orchestrating a theme, in this case literacy: among the letters interspersed throughout Hilary's narrative are ones from this landlady, from Crystal to her 'dull swain' (WC, p. 79) Arthur Fisch, and from Lady Kitty Jopling to Hilary. In their ascending order of literacy these posit, through the particular instance, the difficulty of arriving at general truths about the complexity of the relationship between social standing, intelligence and education. Even Lady Kitty is unable to spell 'providence' and 'psychoanalyst' (WC, p. 170). In general, Murdoch's control over narrative voice and register, either in epistolary form or by means of devices such as the postscripts to The Black Prince, is not always sufficiently appreciated.[61]

The relationship between Hilary and Gunnar is really central to the narrative, clear yet surrounded by mystery. It is reminiscent of, yet different from, familiar forms of the artist–saint contrast: here, as with Henry and Cato (1976), we seem to be watching not so much the artist in one protagonist and the saint in another as a composite of artist and saint in each protagonist, the contrast now lying more explicitly in the social and spiritual circumstances of each protagonist. A reader is prompted, as on previous occasions, to ponder the extent to which the relationship is sublimated and homosexual, with many of the other characters – in this instance Gunnar's two wives particularly – acting as unacknowledged substitutes. Certainly many of the relationships in A Word Child exist in an uneasily shifting equilibrium, different from the cool exchanges of, for instance, A Severed Head; one thinks particularly perhaps of the complex triangle involving Laura Impiatt, Christopher Cather and Clifford Larr. This is comically compounded by Laura's insistences, and Hilary's denials, that Hilary is in love with her: what is characteristic here is what may be thought of as a new uncertainty on the part of the author.

While at Oxford Hilary had precipitated, on his own account, a catastrophe which had ended his and Gunnar's careers there, though Gunnar had subsequently made more of an ostensible 'success' of his life. Hilary, falling desperately in love with Anne, had at last tried to persuade her to leave Gunnar and their young son Tristram. Anne, frightened and confused by her recent discovery that she is once more pregnant, had provoked Hilary into crashing the car on the 'motorway' (a curious anachronism). Hilary had been seriously injured and Anne killed. Much later, Hilary discovers that Gunnar, contrary to what Anne had told him, apparently never knew, or at least had never said to anyone, that she was pregnant. Had she therefore been carrying Hilary's child? The novel provides no answer, though the possibility that she had underlines the humorous potential of the present situation:

> It suddenly struck me as comic . . . that I was now being badgered by three childless women in their thirties, two wanting me to present them with a child, the other wanting me to sanction her marriage. Child-hunger seemed to be the thing just now. (WC, p. 351)

Hilary and Gunnar are both haunted and obsessed by their past, and the extent to which the attempted intermediation of Gunnar's second wife is purely selfless remains doubtful to the reader: Murdoch here skilfully distinguishes between Hilary's fantasy apprehension of and utter trust in Lady Kitty, and a reader's ability to see, as Hilary cannot, the preposterousness of much of her behaviour including her final suggestion that Hilary should provide her with a child. Tristram had earlier committed suicide and Gunnar, as an apparent side-effect of a later operation is, according to Lady Kitty, sterile. Thus Hilary, having already fallen in love with Lady Kitty, appears to be entering compulsively on a course of action identical to that which had earlier proved so destructive. Ironically and disastrously Gunnar, who was supposed to have been away, enters the scene of the last meeting between Hilary and Kitty, in which Hilary had resolved to bring the matter to an end: in a riverside scuffle neither man is injured but Lady Kitty, falling off a jetty, subsequently dies of exposure. Hilary later discovers that he has been unwittingly betrayed by his jealous fiancée Tommy.

The plot is not as mechanical as a summary description makes it sound, since Hilary's compulsive nature is illustrated through the narrative, which is not divided into chapters but arranged as a retrospective 'diary', divided into days, which reflect the rigidness of the only way Hilary seems capable of dealing with his life. The surrounding characters assert their independence surprisingly feebly against Hilary's imposed regime, yet he is capable too of violently spontaneous action, such as ripping the telephone out of the wall. (Telephones are repeatedly invested with nightmare attributes in the Murdoch world.) The status quo of Hilary's life is seen as a series of contrived, repeated actions: crisis is foreshadowed by spontaneity.

Elizabeth Dipple has usefully discussed the relationship between *A Word Child* and J. M. Barrie's *Peter Pan* (1904), a work consistently fascinating to Murdoch and to which there are many allusions in this novel. Dipple has noted that apart from various local decorations the mode of allusion has much to do with the predilection of many of the novel's characters for offering interpretations of *Peter Pan*, frequently as a spiritual allegory.[62] She also draws attention to the functionality, in terms of Hilary's background, served by this and the other pieces of literature he carries around with him 'almost as lucky charms'.[63] It may be thought, too, that in certain respects this novel brings the Shakespearian phase in Murdoch's development to an end, at least in so far as from now on there seems to be a less explicit concern with Shakespearian comic form, and a trend towards a more playful deployment of Shakespearian elements as other interests begin to take on a more dominant role. In *A Word Child*, *King Lear* and Murdoch's reading of that play are present in the comic wantonness of an ending in which Hilary, having resolved to 'sing like birds in the cage' with Crystal (*WC*, p. 383), finds himself in the very next section witnessing her marriage to Arthur. Events in the novel come to support what Hilary has earlier been made to say about his involvement with the Joplings: 'it was not a tragedy. I had not even the consolation of that way of picturing the matter. Tragedy belongs in art. Life has no tragedies' (*WC*, p. 382).

5

'HENRY AND CATO' TO
'THE PHILOSOPHER'S PUPIL'

In the most recent of her novels, Iris Murdoch continues her exploration of the combination of artist and saint in pairs of characters set in opposition. However, she seems now to be paying attention to the backgrounds against which these characters move. Certainly in her latest work there is a new stress on actual as opposed to fictional history, and on the creation and description of frequently highly specific topographical backgrounds other than the hitherto familiar 'Murdochland'. This achievement recalls Murdoch's quest, in the essays published in the late 1950s and early 1960s, for freedom conceived of as portrayal of character against a background of transcendent reality. And, as has already been indicated, in her very latest work the emphasis – from the point of view of Murdoch's sense of available literary tradition – has shifted from Shakespearian comic form towards a contemplation of the nineteenth-century Russian novelists she has for so long admired. Many reviewers of *The Philosopher's Pupil* noted the Karamazov-like relationship between, and personalities of, the McCaffrey brothers, and Dostoevsky seems to lie behind the larger structural preoccupations of this novel. Tolstoy may have been invoked in more local details such as the passage in which a page or so of the action of *The Philosopher's Pupil* is presented through the consciousness of a small dog.

*

The plot of *Henry and Cato* (1976) is so expressly binary that it functions almost as a diptych, and the visual metaphor may reflect the pervasive presence of Max Beckmann in this most painterly of Murdoch's novels. In one panel we observe Henry Marshalson returning from self-imposed academic exile and a ménage à trois in the United States to the ancestral home which he has just inherited on the death in a road accident of his unmarried brother Sandy. During the course of the novel Henry resolves to sell the estate and return to America with Stephanie Whitehouse, who has presented herself in Sandy's London flat as his unacknowledged mistress. A number of circumstances, not least the strong will of Henry's mother Gerda, combine to ensure that this resolve is only partly carried out. In an opposing panel we see Cato Forbes struggling with his priestly vocation in a run-down area of west London and in his relationship to the delinquent youth Beautiful Joe. Cato, too, resolves on a course of renunciation which is only partly achieved. The Forbes and the Marshalsons are long-standing neighbours, and the two panels of the diptych are linked through Cato's sister Colette, whose marriage to Henry at the novel's end characterizes the partial nature of Henry's resolve, since such a marriage has always been Gerda's plan. Cato decides that some of the money which Henry is so anxious to give away can be put to good use by a course of study. Joe, however, rejects Cato once he has renounced the priesthood, and decides on his own course of action. As a result, Henry does ironically give away his money, not out of the phil-anthropy he had resolved on, but in unwittingly conniving at crime: Joe contrives to kidnap first Cato and then Colette, holding them hostage while giving both them and Henry to believe that they are victims of a gang. While about to rape Colette, Joe, not recognized by Cato, is attacked by him and killed.

From a technical point of view there are some new aspects to Murdoch's treatment of the artist–saint contrast; though these are not overwhelming, they do deserve comment. The general march of the plot shows Henry, initially a somewhat fraudulent lecturer in art history at a small Midwest college, returning to dally with philanthropy before settling for a pragmatic solution to the tension between circumstance and principle. Cato, needing to act decisively, is unable to do so until the events which bring about his spontaneous killing of Joe, after which point he has achieved what he needed to achieve but is practically destroyed thereby. Perhaps the major contrast with the novels of the 1950s and 1960s lies in the control exercised over the narrator's handling and presentation of the story. The consciousness of a character such as Gerda is entered into arbitrarily; that of others (such as the bird-headed servant Rhoda) not at all. In addition a character such as the architect Giles Gosling performs a role, previously allocated only to Murdochian letter writers, of being referred to but scarcely entering the narrative's action. The effect of our not seriously discovering Gerda's motivations until relatively late in the action is that new light is thrown towards the end on to the Marshalson panel of the plot; the mess of motives which has led Henry into his relationship with Stephanie (sex, here, too, comes with a twist) can be fully displayed. But it does seem here as though the narrator is less helpful than on previous occasions, not only declining to look consistently into motivations, but undercutting deductions arrived at by the reader; one might say that this narrator displays without revealing, or displays yet manages to preserve the mystery of the characters. This is all in its way a form of realism for Murdoch: it is decorated by arabesques, such as the incomprehensibility of Rhoda, or the graffiti which appear first meaningless then sinister to Cato; these underline the independence of character and narrator. In a more serious way we might think of the ghostly presence of Sandy, which pervades the narrative and the consciousness of the characters. Perhaps we are most inclined to trust Cato's confidant Brendan Craddock, for whom Sandy 'seemed . . . a man filled with desperation' (*HC*, p. 148). Later Henry bursts out, and rightly: 'Everybody around here seems to regard Sandy as the sole fountainhead of significance' (*HC*, p. 292). Recognition of the nature of the symbol-making process, as that part of the consciousness of Murdoch's characters which gives them their distinctiveness as characters, allows a proper response to, say, Cato and his kestrel.

Murdoch's very recent novels demand that the reader should remain relaxed in the face of their complexities. This seems related to her emerging sympathy – evident also from *The Fire and the Sun* (1977) – for the non-acquisitiveness of eastern religious thought in contrast to its western counterpart. She is particularly interested in the way in which Buddhism appears to place so little of Christianity's emphasis on suffering. In a discussion towards the end of *Henry and Cato*, Brendan Craddock, pressed by Cato to say whether he still believes in a personal God, refuses to answer except by making answer impossible by insisting that the notion of God as a person must be a falsification in so far as it is a human picture. That he admits this to be an old sophistry does not detract from Brendan's scrupulousness in seeing death as 'the great destroyer of all images and all stories' which 'human beings will do anything rather than envisage' (*HC*, p. 348). In the light of this scrupulousness it should be possible to see something of what Murdoch means when she writes in *The Fire and the Sun* of a 'strong agile realism' and of the desirability of the work of art being free from the constraints of sentimentality and selfhood.[64] A work of art may of course portray or demonstrate these features while at the same time revealing their inadequacy.

*

The Sea, The Sea (1978) continues to explore the theme of renunciation and, like *Henry and Cato*, to do so by means of a binary opposition involving artist and saint. Charles Arrowby, the narrator, more than once identified with Prospero, has just retired from a successful career as a theatrical director and has bought a retreat, Shruff End, on an unnamed and barren piece of the British coastline. His attempts to remain in solitude are thwarted by the arrival of various visitors, with whom he is compelled to share the lonely delights of the land-and seascape. (The title refers not only to Xenophon but more relevantly to Paul Valéry's 'Le Cimetière marin', a poem of constant interest to Murdoch, and explicitly to the line: '*La mer, la mer, toujours recommencée!*') Among Charles's visitors is his cousin James, an ex-soldier, to whom Charles has always felt inferior. James, too, it later transpires, has been attempting a renunciation by coming to detach himself from Charles and, indeed, from life: later, in the manner of an eastern adept, he apparently wills himself to die. However, though he is ostensibly sympathetic to Buddhism, Murdoch has in a recent interview referred to him as a 'lost soul'.[65] Like Charles, James is forced back into involvement with the world he wishes to leave when it emerges towards the end of the book that by an exercise of paranormal power he has earlier saved Charles's life. Charles has hitherto been amnesiac about the details of his rescue from the lethally dangerous whirlpool into which he had been pushed.

Both James's powers and Charles's theatrical techniques are referred to during the novel as 'tricks', and one of the matters emerging from the narrative has to do with the clash between the ease of deciding on a course of renunciation and the difficulty of actually achieving it. Murdoch has additionally suggested that James is in love with Charles, so that James's attempts to detach himself are considerably more fraught than they appear on the surface. The chosen narrative mode renders verification of the nature of the relationship impossible, since Charles's perceptions frequently cannot be relied upon, and James remains largely opaque. Though there are conversations between the two men, and their relationship is in its general essence a familiar one, there is nothing equivalent in *The Sea, The Sea* to the reparative discussions between Jake and Hugo in *Under the Net*.

Among Charles's other visitors are the servile Gilbert Opian (a familiar Murdoch type), whose arrival ushers in a period of relative stability as he keeps house for Charles, and Rosina Vambrugh, one of Charles's ex-mistresses, whose attentions are far more demonic. Before she actually appears on the scene, she has apparently been in the house, breaking and damaging various objects, but her presence, once admitted, does not account for all the poltergeistlike goings on. As is later asserted, the house has 'bad vibes' (*TSTS*, p. 313). In the main section of the book, 'History', Charles's most serious crisis is not, however, these visitations but his discovery that his boyhood love Mary Hartley, whom he has not seen since, is living in the village, less than happily married to a man named Ben Fitch. Charles's extraordinary resolve to 'free' her and keep her captive at Shruff End recalls episodes involving *princesses lointaines* in other novels, and to some extent anticipates John Robert Rozanov's attitude to his granddaughter in *The Philosopher's Pupil*. Charles discovers the existence of Ben and Hartley's adopted son Titus, who reappears after having been missing for two years and joins the visitors. Charles, flattered by the mysterious way in which Titus has come to visit him, and anxious to use him as 'bait' in luring Hartley to Shruff End, fails to warn him adequately of the dangers of the sea, and Titus is eventually drowned.

Charles is never able to ascertain whether James had previously known Titus, but James is curiously distressed by the accident, as though he had foreseen and were in some way responsible for it. In the last, strangely opaque conversation between the two men, once James's paranormal powers have been admitted, it transpires that James had once caused a death by similarly overestimating his ability: crossing a Tibetan pass with a young Sherpa, he had thought that he could keep both of them alive by the exercise of raising the body temperature. Both men's failures come to be seen as a form of hubris and serve to link them yet more closely. The distress which James shows at Charles's failure to warn Titus of the sea reminds us of the pain so often brought about by the (by now familiar) obsessively repeated destructive action. But it is the vicarious effect of this particular repetition which is curiously characteristic of recent Murdoch.

For there is unusual emphasis in *The Sea, The Sea* on the

identification of people with each other or – put another way – on the fluidity of the boundaries separating people; this helps make sense of the supernatural happenings,[66] some of which are clustered together in energetic groups which constantly force us to question Charles's reliability as narrator. Early in the book Charles sees a face peering through a window separating two rooms at an unusual height. This vision is recalled after a dream later on, when Hartley is captive in the house. In his dream Charles enters Hartley's room:

> Hartley was gone – I stared about, ready to cry out with panic fear. And then I saw her – she was standing in the corner. I thought, how odd I had forgotten how tall she is. Then I thought she is standing on something, how odd, she must be up on the chair or the table. Then I saw that she was suspended from the lamp bracket. She had hanged herself.
> (*TSTS*, p. 309)

Charles awakes in relief to find that this was a dream, but is then very disconcerted to remember that in his earlier vision the height of the face he had glimpsed would exactly coincide with that of the hanged Hartley. That this is not restricted to Charles's mind may be realized when we recall apparently meaningless reminiscences shared by Hartley and Titus *after* the earlier vision; a recurrent part of these reminiscences refers to Titus standing on a box to see over the fence in their garden. Later, Charles remembers this when he breaks into the Fitches' deserted house. Memory clusters such as these internal echoes are invested with demonic and possibly fatal energy which can work backwards and forwards in time, yet they are also relativized by our reservations concerning Charles's reliability. Finally, a certain doubt is cast even on the centrality of Hartley's existence in Charles's life in the 'Postscript: Life Goes On', and it might be said that this novel, in addition to all its other riches and patterns, consistently plays with the motto: '*on n'aime qu'une fois, la première*'.

*

91

Nuns and Soldiers (1980), though bearing the hallmark of Murdoch's mature style and thought, it possibly the least effective of these novels. It might be thought of as a peripheral version of *Hamlet* in that it invites us to contemplate that play from an unconventional angle. There is no reluctant revenger, but there is a pub called The Prince of Denmark in which revenge is rather wildly spoken of. Stress falls on Gertrude Openshaw's remarriage at the behest of her husband Guy, who is dying of cancer. James Arrowby might well have thought of Guy's wish as the kind of 'less than perfect meddling in the spiritual world [which] can breed monsters for other people' (*TSTS*, pp. 445, 471); certainly the remarriage is looked on with disfavour by much of the bourgeois court constituted by Guy's relations. Tim Reede, the second husband, is a painter of dubious talent and character on the periphery of this court, given to raiding the Openshaws' fridge during drinks and returning to his mistress Daisy Barrett with the spoils. Yet the marriage, after surviving a purgatorial period, is worked at, and at this level the story is very much one of settling for imperfections.

The title caused some puzzlement among reviewers as there is only ostensibly one nun in the book (and she is introduced after having left the cloister) and no soldier but a devotee of military history. It would be consistent with Murdoch's thought, however, for the title to refer to the ways people see themselves and others. Although there are some innovations, largely from the point of view of technique, there is a great deal that is familiar and which begins – as at other times in Murdoch's career – to look like self-parody. The 'ex-nun' Anne Cavidge is unrequitedly in love with the Polish 'Count' (Wojciech Szczepanski); he is unrequitedly in love with Gertrude. There is suffering, deceit, drink and fatigue. But it is worth dwelling for a moment on the innovations, since it is not at all certain how unconsciously introduced the apparently familiar features are. Murdoch seems to be treading a highly difficult path here as she attempts to incorporate into the narrative so much that is quotidian and of seemingly dubious 'relevance'. The effort put into the 'technical excursions' of earlier novels has recently been transferred to the creation of other kinds of wilfully 'irrelevant' but marvellously noticed description. Murdoch seems to have abandoned altogether the Jamesian centre-of-consciousness narrative in favour of frank omniscience ('What Manfred was thinking will be revealed later' (NS, p. 144)).

Anne Cavidge's vision of Jesus Christ presents the book's greatest challenge in the context of omniscience, since the narrator is anxious to insist that it was not a dream, and it leaves a stigma on Anne's hand which cannot be healed. Characteristic of the vision is its iconoclasm, and it seems to me that Murdoch's conviction, that religious experience is deceptive if it relies too much on preconceived images, is consistent with the stress placed in this novel on peripherality. Anne's migraine may be a figure for this:

> She had entirely lost the centre of her field of vision. The centre was occupied by a large greyish round hole into which she seemed to stare, round the edge of which was a fringe of boiling particles not unlike porridge. Outside this the edges of the field of vision, what is seen 'out of the corner of the eye', appeared as usual. (NS, p. 391)

Only when the centre is blacked out can attention be paid to what lies on the edges. This truth is distilled towards the end of the book in a revealing conversation between two of the characters, Manfred and Mrs Mount, members of the court of 'les cousins et les tantes', who have been only marginally present in the narrative so far. Their conversation is concluded by the arrival of the elusive Balintoy. This strengthens our sense that the story could have been told another way. Attention is paid to the edges, while respect is retained for their integrity *as* edges.

Nuns and Soldiers represents a departure from Murdochian convention in its sense of history. The Count, though Polish, has absolutely nothing of the feyness of the Lusiewicz brothers, and indeed his own historical consciousness is connected to our sense of this novel's being the most closely related – of the entire Murdoch canon – to the time in which it was written. Towards the end an allusion to the accession of a Polish pope may allow us to feel that a real historical event took a hand in shaping the development of a fiction. With the exception of *The Red and the Green*, there is nowhere else in Murdoch's fiction such reference to historical dates. We may recall that Murdoch's more usual policy with dates which could 'place' a fiction in historical time is to subvert and distract, as with the treatment of the Boases in *Bruno's Dream* (reference to Will Boase in *The Sea, The Sea* subverts matters further).

*

These recent novels, although allowing us to feel that Murdoch may not be willing to do much more to surprise her readers, none the less continue to highlight her subtle and complex understanding of realism. She is scrupulous about the senses in which the novel should and should not be mimetic of human experience. The 'baroque' and 'mandarin' have a place in Murdoch's fictional world, and one which is frequently mistaken for sympathetic indulgence. Yet to show the respects in which the human mind may indulge itself is necessarily to deal attentively with those respects. It is significant that many readers and reviewers of *The Fire and the Sun*, while commending its lucid exposition of Plato's thought, were uncertain to what extent Murdoch was refuting or sympathizing with it, and were able to note how fascinating she found the paradoxical coexistence of puritan and artist in Plato.

The latest novel to date, *The Philosopher's Pupil* (1983), raises these matters once more, and does so in the context of two further departures from established Murdochian convention. This novel is technically a first-person narration which, instead of being that of a character whose own role in the story is thereby revealed in an unconsciously uncomplimentary fashion, performs in effect the function of an omniscient third-person narration. The narrator of *The Philosopher's Pupil*, N, never identifies himself beyond saying 'I am a shadow, Nemo, not the masked presence or secret voice of one of the main characters' (*PP*, p. 16). Every other first-person Murdochian narration depends for at least some of its effect on what the narrator reveals himself not to have known: here, N knows even more than any third-person narrator in the Murdoch canon about the details of the story he is telling. Indeed, he is a great deployer of fussy parenthetic detail, incorporating material (the menu of a beach picnic, the lyrics of an excruciatingly bad pop song) which no reader can possibly need or even want to know. Imagining himself, at the 'arbitrarily determined' end of his story, being asked: 'But how on earth do you know all these things about all these people?', N replies: 'Well, where does one person end and another begin? It is my role in life to listen to stories. I also had the assistance of a certain lady' (*PP*, p. 576).

The second major departure from established convention, although it does now reflect interestingly on the Anglo-Jewish clannishness of '*les cousins et les tantes*' in *Nuns and Soldiers*, lies in the topographical background to *The Philosopher's Pupil*. The 'Murdochland' of south-west London has been completely abandoned here; the action of the novel takes place entirely in a spa town within commuting distance of London, which N refers to as 'Ennistone'. The town and its baths are described in the second of two prefatory sections in minute – almost guidebook – detail and seem not to be of obligatory, conscripted relevance to the story but, on the contrary, of equal interest to N as the story itself. (The main section is entitled 'The Events in Our Town'.) It is also worth pointing out that *The Philosopher's Pupil* is longer, and its cast larger, than any of its predecessors. (During its course we learn of the death of Hugo Belfounder; the speaker imparting this information is unable to remember the name of 'that writer' (*PP*, p. 95).)

The philosopher, John Robert Rozanov, one of Ennistone's most distinguished townsmen, returns with his orphaned granddaughter Hattie Meynell and her 'maid' Pearl Scotney. Only later in the novel does it become clear that the major purpose of the visit was Rozanov's Prospero-like wish that

Hattie should surrender her virginity in marriage to a suitable young man. Rozanov selects Tom McCaffrey, a student at London University, whose half-brothers George and Brian and stepmother Alex are residents of Ennistone. (At one point Rozanov, who does not read novels, discovers a copy of *Les Liaisons Dangereuses* (1782) in Hattie's possession, and one view of his intentions may suggest similarities with Choderlos de Laclos rather than with Shakespeare.) Tom bungles the philosopher's instructions that matters should be undertaken with the utmost propriety and discretion, and is at first rejected by Hattie. Later, there is an unseemly revel, involving most of the cast of an amateur production of a masque called *The Triumph of Aphrodite*, in the garden of the Slipper House (situated in the grounds of Alex's house, Belmont), which Rozanov has rented for the girls. This un-*Merchant of Venice*-like scene ('In such a night as this') is scandalously reported in a local gossip column. Almost overcome with rage, Rozanov removes Hattie from the Slipper House and from Pearl (whom he believes to be a vicious accomplice), and reluctantly reveals his true motive for having wished to arrange Hattie's marriage: he is in love with her. Tom, having meanwhile almost miraculously overcome an ordeal in which he was apparently accidentally shut in the steamy depths of the hot springs while its workings were being investigated, returns to claim Hattie.

It might be thought from the summary so far that Tom is the 'pupil' of the novel's title, and indeed the teacher–pupil relationship echoes subordinately in the detailed portrayals of the eccentric priest, Father Bernard Jacoby, enlisted by Rozanov as tutor to Hattie, and Mr Hanway, singing teacher to Tom's companion Emma (Emmanuel Scarlett-Taylor). However, one of the major structuring principles of the narrative is provided by the repeated attempts of George McCaffrey, a former pupil of Rozanov's, to re-establish contact with him, and his continual rejection by Rozanov. Finally George, about whose sanity there is constant debate in the narrative, decides to kill Rozanov, and pays a last visit to the rooms which Rozanov has hired at Ennistone's baths. Here, as on a previous occasion,

George discovers Rozanov asleep, but this time drowns him (and his book) in his bath. This, George's final action in the book, exerts an intensifying effect on his first, the subject of the novel's first prefatory section ('An Accident'). Here George, driving home with his wife Stella from drinks with Alex, has a 'brainstorm, or whatever it was' (*PP*, p. 1) and is afterwards never sure whether he drove or pushed the car into the canal and tried deliberately to drown Stella. Father Bernard, who had witnessed the attempted drowning of Stella, is just too late to intercept George before the drowning of Rozanov. But he does discover among Rozanov's papers the suicide note which George had missed. From this it seems that Rozanov must have been irrecoverably comatose, if not actually dead, when George immersed him. The two drowning episodes taken together represent what is characteristic of this narrative, and throw more light on how Murdoch visualizes fictional realism. The uncertainties surrounding George's actions resonate together and confuse any possible 'solution', *despite, and probably because of*, N's obsessive way with information. N does not discriminate in the way characteristic of the 'crystalline' novelist whose preconceptions Murdoch censured earlier in her career, yet his narrative retains a form which is not 'journalistic'. A number of characteristically Murdochian episodes with symbolic potential, such as George's rescuing his nephew Adam's dog Zed from the sea, or Tom's descent into the steamy depths beneath the baths, are flamboyantly displayed yet resist easy symbolic interpretation; N delights instead in their details. Similarly, the interpretative relevance of works of art whose titles are embedded in the narrative is more potentially ambivalent than ever before (though of course their occurrence as such is not new in Murdoch). They are no longer left around, as it were, as 'keys', but serve now primarily to decorate, as do the trio of gipsy ladies, Pearl, Ruby (Alex's maid) and Diane (née Diamond, George's mistress), whose relationship to each other is left obscure, though they are described as 'cousins'. Perhaps the difficulty here is most economically pointed to by musing on the relationship between two little episodes of confrontation which ask to be taken as paralleling each other but, like George's actions, simply seem to resonate against each other. The dog Zed's consciousness is entered into briefly at one stage in the garden at Belmont as he confronts one of the foxes that inhabit it. This seems to anticipate a moment of climax during the *Triumph of Aphrodite* revels in which George gets into the Slipper House and is seen (by N) advancing on a solitary Hattie before she has the presence of mind to pull the blinds back and be seen by the revellers. In both, a frail 'crushable' innocence is confronted by an anarchistic force apparently outside conventional human norms – and then nothing happens: the everyday world resumes control, the dangerous, almost numinous, moment is over.

*

Iris Murdoch's understanding of what it means to be a contemporary writer is an intensely personal one, and it has been achieved through a profound and articulate understanding of the relationship between art and morality in the context of the historical moment in which she lives. She has given serious and extended thought to the difficulties underlying the whole enterprise of writing fiction in an age and culture which evinces highly ambivalent attitudes towards 'greatness' in art and which has become deeply suspicious of the kind of liberal creative impulse which she herself possesses. She has discerned – as have few other contemporary thinkers – the extent of paradox inherent in a situation in which art-works of whatever kind can become grand, available and iconic, and can at the same time be held, humbly and unassertively, to provide 'work for the spirit'. It is in the context of her distrust for the thinking entailed in this paradox that we should see her attainment of a frankly ritualistic form of fantasy realism.

Looking back over her career as a novelist, and knowingly detecting her allotropic repetition of theme and situation, we may choose to settle for accusing her of indulgence and self-parody. But closer examination of her assured, inventive attention to detail may allow us to discern a real alertness to the attractive dangers of artistic form. Not all her contemporaries share her assessment of the problems of writing fiction in Britain today, and even among those who may be felt to respect it, not all react in the same way to what it embodies. We may think of William Golding as a writer whose scrupulous response to what he sees as a temptation to write derivatively or repetitively is to devise alien contexts and settings for his fiction, and, if necessary, to remain silent. A response rather more characteristic of the novelist in Britain today may be that of Angus Wilson, a writer who, only too well aware of the extent of the achievement which precedes him, is able to draw strength from his parodic engagement with a voraciously assimilated tradition of fiction. Wilson's neo-Forsterian liberal inheritance may invite superficial comparison with Murdoch, but her particular combination of intellect and temperament have led her, in her novels, towards an increasingly characteristic and subtle conception of the appropriate combination of form and contingency. She is not afraid to employ through her narrators a tone of melodramatic intensification to represent the agonized states of mind of those who have submitted to the charm of fantasy (this is to be thought of as a recurrent, yet for each sufferer a unique, experience), and she can use the resources of fictional form to enact its own subversion. She is fully aware that, in the most technically gifted hands, and through the eyes of the artist most ready to imagine the free, separate existence of human beings who are not himself, the novel may be a profoundly liberating form:

> Anne had been reading *Little Dorrit*, it was amazing, it was so crammed and chaotic, and yet so touching, a kind of miracle, a strangely naked display of feeling, and full of profound ideas, and yet one felt it was all true! (*NS*, p. 54)

Murdoch is, in short, a writer who is not afraid to take risks, and she writes as she does not out of a sense of bizarre hubristic carelessness, but as a necessary consequence of reaching still more closely towards the creation of the kind of novel for which she has constantly pleaded. Offering as it does 'a strangely naked display of feeling', her best work runs the major risk of being underrated through coarse-grained comparison with the tradition of whose greatness she has been a tireless advocate; yet it is characteristic of her modesty and moral sense that she should expose herself to this risk knowing what is involved. The reviewer of *The Philosopher's Pupil* who wrote of its combination of Dostoevsky and soap opera may have offered a greater compliment than he realized. The repository of greatness on which contemporary writers can draw has perhaps become, like Anne Cavidge's vision, reduced and curiously familiar, but responses to it may need to become increasingly iconoclastic and, by this token, may contain obscure dangers. Yet it is still available *as* a repository, and Iris Murdoch has not shrunk from its touch.

NOTES

1 Heide Ziegler and Christopher Bigsby (eds), *The Radical Imagination and the Liberal Tradition* (London: Junction Books, 1982), p. 212.

2 Blake Morrison, *The Movement* (London: Oxford University Press, 1980), pp. 2, 245, refers to J. D. Scott's pioneer inclusion of *Under the Net* with the first novels of Kingsley Amis and John Wain (*Spectator*, 1 October 1954), and notes that *The Sandcastle* contains 'Movement elements' in its provincial school environment.

3 This information has been abstracted from data kindly supplied by Chatto & Windus Ltd.

4 Iris Murdoch, 'Important Things' (review of Simone de Beauvoir, *The Mandarins*), *The Sunday Times*, 17 February 1957.

5 For a recent formulation of this conviction, see Bryan Magee (ed.), *Men of Ideas* (London: BBC Publications, 1978), pp. 274–5.

6 Iris Murdoch, 'The Sublime and the Beautiful Revisited', *Yale Review*, 49 (1959), p. 260.

7 See John Haffenden, 'In Conversation with Iris Murdoch', *Literary Review/Quarto*, 58 (April 1983), pp. 31–4.

8 Frank Kermode, 'The House of Fiction', *Partisan Review*, 30 (1963), pp. 61–82; repr. in Malcolm Bradbury (ed.), *The Novel Today* (London: Fontana/Collins, 1977), p. 115.

9 Michael Bellamy, 'An Interview with Iris Murdoch', *Wisconsin Studies in Contemporary Literature*, 18 (1977), p. 135.

10 Malcolm Bradbury, 'Iris Murdoch in Conversation with Malcolm Bradbury', recorded 27 February 1976, British Council tape no. RS 2001.

11 Iris Murdoch, 'Against Dryness', *Encounter*, 16 (January 1961), pp. 16–20; repr. in Bradbury (ed.), 1977, op. cit., p. 29.

12 Kermode, op. cit., p. 115.

13 Murdoch, 'The Sublime and the Beautiful Revisited', p. 271.

14 Bradbury, 1976, op. cit.

15 The phrase is used in Kermode, op. cit., p. 118.

16 W. K. Rose, 'Iris Murdoch, Informally', *London Magazine*, 8 (June 1968), pp. 59–70.

17 Bradbury, 1976, op. cit.

18 The description is Murdoch's own; see Ziegler and Bigsby (eds), op. cit., p. 229.

19 Ibid., p. 227.

20 Frank Kermode, 'Novels of Iris Murdoch', *Spectator*, 7 November 1958, p. 618.

21 Iris Murdoch, 'The Sublime and the Good', *Chicago Review*, 13 (1959), p. 51.

22 Ibid, p. 52.

23 A. S. Byatt, *Iris Murdoch* (London: Longman, 1976), pp. 23–4.

24 Murdoch, 'The Sublime and the Beautiful Revisited', p. 266.

25 Murdoch, 'Against Dryness', p. 26.

26 See Murdoch, 'The Sublime and the Beautiful Revisited', p. 265, where she identifies de Beauvoir's *The Mandarins* as 'journalistic' and Camus's *The Stranger* as 'crystalline'; and Murdoch, 'Against Dryness', p. 27. The distinction was to her 'epigrammatic' and 'probably . . . rather inexact' by the time of 'The House of Fiction' interview (1963) (Bradbury (ed.), 1977, op. cit., p. 113).

27 Murdoch, 'The Sublime and the Beautiful Revisited', p. 271.

28 Ronald Bryden, review in *Spectator*, 16 June 1961, p. 885.

29 Cyril Connolly, review in *The Sunday Times*, 18 June 1961.

30 Raymond Queneau, review in *Time and Tide*, 6 July 1961, p. 1119.

31 Rose, op. cit., p. 60.

32 D. W. Harding, 'The Novels of Iris Murdoch', *Oxford Magazine*, 26 October 1961, p. 34.

33 Iris Murdoch, *The Sovereignty of Good* (London: Oxford University Press, 1970), p. 51.

34 Robert Scholes, *Fabulation and Metafiction* (Urbana and Chicago, Ill., and London: University of Illinois Press, 1979), p. 68.

35 Ruth Heyd, 'An Interview with Iris Murdoch', *University of Windsor Review*, 1 (1965), p. 142.

36 Scholes, op. cit., p. 66.

37 Elizabeth Dipple, *Iris Murdoch: Work for the Spirit* (London: Methuen, 1982), p. 152.

38 This is confirmed by recent remarks; see Jean-Louis Chevalier (ed.), *Rencontres avec Iris Murdoch* (Caen, France: Centre de

Recherches de Littérature et Linguistique des Pays de Langue Anglaise, 1978), p. 92.

39 See Louis L. Martz, 'Iris Murdoch: The London Novels', in Reuben A. Brower (ed.), *Twentieth-Century Literature in Retrospect* (Cambridge, Mass.: Harvard University Press, 1971), pp. 65–86.

40 Murdoch, *The Sovereignty of Good*, p. 55.

41 *The times Literary Supplement* (anon. review), 8 September 1966, p. 798. It is interesting to note that Murdoch adduces Verkhovensky, together with Shallow and Silence, as instances of 'one of the greatest achievements of all' in art, which is 'to join [a] sense of absolute mortality not to the tragic but to the comic' (*The Sovereignty of Good*, p. 87).

42 A. S. Byatt, review in *New Statesman*, 26 January 1968, pp. 113–14.

43 The word is William F. Hall's in '*Bruno's Dream*: Technique and Meaning in the Novels of Iris Murdoch', *Modern Fiction Studies*, 15 (1969), p. 443, though his assessment of *The Time of the Angels* is more favourable than mine.

44 These and other elements are catalogued by Peter Kemp, 'The Fight against Fantasy: Iris Murdoch's *The Red and the Green*', *Modern Fiction Studies*, 15 (1969), pp. 412–15. But see also Christopher Ricks, 'A Sort of Mystery Novel', *New Statesman*, 22 October 1965, pp. 604–5 and 'The Daisychain of Passion', *The Sunday Times*, 7 September 1980.

45 The exigencies of the present undertaking compel me to play down the Shakespearian elements in these novels in favour of concerns which I was less able to notice in *Iris Murdoch: The Shakespearian Interest* (London: Vision, 1979).

46 Murdoch, *The Sovereignty of Good*, p. 87.

47 A. S. Byatt, review in the *New Statesman*, 17 January 1969, p. 86.

48 Frank Kermode, 'Iris Murdoch', in his *Modern Essays* (London: Fontana/Collins, 1971), p. 264.

49 Lorna Sage, 'The Pursuit of Imperfection', *Critical Quarterly*, 19 (1977), p. 66.

50 Murdoch, *The Sovereignty of Good*, p. 68.

51 Ibid., p. 87.

52 See Bellamy, op. cit., pp. 135–6. In Chevalier (ed.), op. cit., pp. 75–6, Murdoch expands on this scheme and defends the novel against charges of anti-semitism.

53 Iris Murdoch, 'The Moral Decision about Homosexuality', *Man and Society*, 7 (1964), p. 5.

54 The word is borrowed from Frank Kermode's review of *Henry and Cato* in *The Guardian*, 30 September 1976.

55 Iris Murdoch, 'Salvation by Words', *New York Review of Books*, 15 June 1972, p. 4. In an unpublished radio interview with A. S. Byatt, 'Now Read On', 27 October 1971, Murdoch also adduced the instance of Pieter Breughel's 'Icarus' and W. H. Auden's celebrated description of it in 'Musée des Beaux Arts'.

56 Iris Murdoch, in Cecil Woolf and John Bagguley (eds), *Authors Take Sides on Vietnam* (London: Owen, 1967), p. 40.

57 See Iris Murdoch's interview with Ronald Hayman, 'Out of the Tutorial', *The Times*, 30 September 1970.

58 Murdoch specifies that the General is to be played by the same actor who plays a gipsy, Patrice, and this seems a reminiscence of *Peter Pan* where J. M. Barrie has Mr Darling and Captain Hook similarly linked. Murdoch is manifestly attracted not only to the Barrie play but also to this kind of allusive quirk; see Chevalier (ed.), op. cit., p. 86.

59 Byatt, 1976, op. cit., p. 37. Unlike Byatt, I am stressing the possibility that *both* characters might represent elements relevant to Murdoch's artistic make-up. Possibly Baffin is to be seen as the more conscious, and Pearson the more unconscious, element. See the recent comments in Chevalier (ed.), op. cit., p. 78.

60 Iris Murdoch, 'Socialism and Selection', in C. B. Cox and Rhodes Boyson (eds), *Black Paper 1975* (London: Dent, 1975), p. 9.

61 A footnote is perhaps the proper place to suggest that a critic such as Ricks (see note 44), while wittily castigating mannerisms ('a sort of XY') in, for instance, *Nuns and Soldiers*, is explicitly – and surely perversely – failing to distinguish between the narrator's voice and the registers of the various characters. I am not denying the presence of such mannerisms nor claiming that they never irritate, but Ricks never admits the possibility that they may be (whether consciously or unconsciously) performing a function which might be conceived of in other terms than as simply acting as formulae for authorial inexactness. Moreover, Murdoch has rigorously distinguished, not just between the kind of activity, but between the uses of language, proper to philosopher and novelist: the former involves one in 'purification of one's statements', whereas the artistic 'reshaping' of form out of experience may involve 'offences against truth' (Magee, op. cit., pp. 265, 266). As Ricks points out, *Nuns and Soldiers* is indeed a novel much concerned with lying; as he conspicuously fails to point out, he is censuring its style for not doing something Murdoch has claimed it cannot do.

62 Dipple, op. cit., pp. 216–17.

63 Ibid., p. 217.

64 Iris Murdoch, *The Fire and the Sun* (London: Oxford University Press, 1977), p. 84.
65 Ziegler and Bigsby (eds), op. cit., p. 213.
66 Dipple (op. cit., p. 278 and elsewhere) is surely right to pursue connections between the sea monster seen by Charles, his jealousy, and his apprehensions not only of James but of several other characters too.

BIBLIOGRAPHY

WORKS BY IRIS MURDOCH

Novels

Under the Net. London: Chatto & Windus, 1954. New York: Viking Press, 1954.

The Flight from the Enchanter. London: Chatto & Windus, 1956. New York: Viking Press, 1956.

The Sandcastle. London: Chatto & Windus, 1957. New York: Viking Press, 1957.

The Bell. London: Chatto & Windus, 1958. New York: Viking Press, 1958.

A Severed Head. London: Chatto & Windus, 1961. New York: Viking Press, 1961.

An Unofficial Rose. London: Chatto & Windus, 1962. New York: Viking Press, 1962.

The Unicorn. London: Chatto & Windus, 1963. New York: Viking Press, 1963.

The Italian Girl. London: Chatto & Windus, 1964. New York: Viking Press, 1964.

The Red and the Green. London: Chatto & Windus, 1965. New York: Viking Press, 1965.

The Time of the Angels. London: Chatto & Windus, 1966. New York: Viking Press, 1966.

The Nice and the Good. London: Chatto & Windus, 1968. New York: Viking Press, 1968.

Bruno's Dream. London: Chatto & Windus, 1969. New York: Viking Press, 1969.

A Fairly Honourable Defeat. London: Chatto & Windus, 1970. New York: Viking Press, 1970.

An Accidental Man. London: Chatto & Windus, 1971. New York: Viking Press, 1971.

The Black Prince. London: Chatto & Windus, 1973. New York: Viking Press, 1973.

The Sacred and Profane Love Machine. London: Chatto & Windus, 1974. New York: Viking Press, 1974.

A Word Child. London: Chatto & Windus, 1975. New York: Viking Press, 1975.

Henry and Cato. London: Chatto & Windus, 1976. New York: Viking Press, 1977.

The Sea, The Sea. London: Chatto & Windus, 1978. New York: Viking Press, 1978.

Nuns and Soldiers. London: Chatto & Windus, 1980. New York: Viking Press, 1981.

The Philosopher's Pupil. London: Chatto & Windus, 1983. New York: Viking Press, 1983.

Short story

'Something Special'. In *Winter's Tales*, Vol. 3, pp. 175–204. London: Macmillan, 1957. New York: St Martin's Press, 1957.

Plays

A Severed Head (with J. B. Priestley). London: Chatto & Windus, 1964.

The Italian Girl (with James Saunders). London and New York: Samuel French, 1968.

The Three Arrows and *The Servants and the Snow*. London: Chatto & Windus, 1973. New York: Viking Press, 1974.

The Servants (adaptation of *The Servants and the Snow* as libretto for the opera by William Mathias). London: Oxford University Press Music Dept, 1980.

Poetry

'Agamemnon Class 1939'. *Boston University Journal*, 25, 2 (1977), pp. 57–8.

'Poem and Egg', 'The Brown Horse', 'The Public Garden in Calimera'. *Transatlantic Review*, 60 (June 1977), pp. 31–4.

'Motorist and Dead Bird'. *The Listener*, 16 June 1977, p. 781.

A Year of Birds (with engravings by Reynolds Stone). Tisbury, Wilts: Compton Press, 1978.

'Too Late', 'Fox', 'No Smell', 'Gunnera', 'Edible Fungi'. *Poetry London Apple Magazine*, 1, 1 (Autumn 1979), pp. 38–42.

'The Novelist as Metaphysician'. *The Listener*, 16 March 1950, pp. 473–6.

'The Existentialist Hero'. *The Listener*, 23 March 1950, pp. 523–4.

'The Existentialist Political Myth'. *The Socratic*, 5 (1952), pp. 52–63.

'Nostalgia for the Particular'. *Proceedings of the Aristotelian Society*, 52 (1952), pp. 243–60.

Sartre: Romantic Rationalist. Cambridge: Bowes & Bowes, 1953. New Haven, Conn.: Yale University Press, 1953. London: Fontana/Collins, 1967. 2nd edn, Brighton: Harvester Press, 1980. New York: Barnes & Noble, 1980.

'Vision and Choice in Morality (ii)'. In *Dreams and Self-Knowledge*. Aristotelian Society Supplementary Volume 30, pp. 32–58. London: Harrison, 1956.

'Knowing the Void'. *Spectator*, 2 November 1956, pp. 613–14.

'Important Things' (review of Simone de Beauvoir, *The Mandarins*). *The Sunday Times*, 17 February 1957.

'Hegel in Modern Dress'. *New Statesman*, 25 May 1957, p. 675.

'Metaphysics and Ethics'. In D. F. Pears (ed.), *The Nature of Metaphysics*, pp. 99–123. London: Macmillan, 1957. New York: St Martin's Press, 1957.

'T. S. Eliot as a Moralist'. In Neville Braybrooke (ed.), *T. S. Eliot: A Symposium for his Seventieth Birthday*, pp. 152–60. London: Rupert Hart-Davis, 1958. New York: Farrar, Straus & Cudahy, 1958.

'A House of Theory'. *Partisan Review*, 26 (1959), pp. 17–31.

'The Sublime and the Beautiful Revisited'. *Yale Review*, 49 (1959), pp. 247–71.

'The Sublime and the Good'. *Chicago Review,* 13 (1959), pp. 42–55.

'Negative Capability'. *Adam International Review*, 284–6 (1960), pp. 172–3.

'Against Dryness'. *Encounter*, 16 (January 1961), pp. 16–20. Repr. in Malcolm Bradbury (ed.), *The Novel Today*, pp. 23–31. London: Fontana/Collins, 1977.

'Mass, Might and Myth' (review of Elias Canetti, *Crowds and Power*). *Spectator*, 7 September 1962, pp. 337–8.

'Speaking of Writing'. *The Times*, 13 February 1964.

'The Moral Decision about Homosexuality'. *Man and Society*, 7 (1964), pp. 3–6.

'The Darkness of Practical Reason'. *Encounter*, 27 (July 1966), pp. 46–50.

'Political Morality'. *The Listener*, 21 September 1967, pp. 353–4.

Contribution to Cecil Woolf and John Bagguley (eds), *Authors Take Sides on Vietnam*, p. 40. London: Owen, 1967.

'Existentialists and Mystics'. In W. W. Robson (ed.), *Essays and Poems Presented to Lord David Cecil*, pp. 169–83. London: Constable, 1970.

The Sovereignty of Good. London: Oxford University Press, 1970. New York: Schocken Books, 1971. (Includes 'The Idea of Perfection' (1964), 'The Sovereignty of Good over Other Concepts' (1967) and 'On "God" and "Good"' (1969).)

'Salvation by Words'. *New York Review of Books*, 15 June 1972, pp. 3–6.

'Socialism and Selection'. In C. B. Cox and Rhodes Boyson (eds), *Black Paper 1975*, pp. 7–9. London: Dent, 1975.

The Fire and the Sun: Why Plato Banished the Artists. London: Oxford University Press, 1977.

'Art is the Imitation of Nature'. *Cahiers du Centre de Recherches sur les Pays du Nord et du Nord-Ouest*, 1 (1978), pp. 59–65.

SELECTED CRITICISM OF IRIS MURDOCH

Books

Baldanza, Frank. *Iris Murdoch*. New York: Twayne, 1974.

Byatt, A. S. *Degrees of Freedom: The Novels of Iris Murdoch*. London: Chatto & Windus, 1965. New York: Barnes & Noble, 1965.

—— *Iris Murdoch*. London: Longman, 1976.

Chevalier, Jean-Louis (ed.). *Rencontres avec Iris Murdoch*. Caen, France: Centre de Recherches de Littérature et Linguistique des Pays de Langue Anglaise, 1978.

Dipple, Elizabeth. *Iris Murdoch: Work for the Spirit*. London: Methuen, 1982. Chicago, Ill.: University of Chicago Press, 1982.

Gerstenberger, Donna. *Iris Murdoch*. Lewisburg, Pa: Bucknell University Press, 1975. London: Associated University Presses, 1975.

Rabinovitz, Rubin. *Iris Murdoch*. New York: Columbia University Press, 1968. Repr. in George Stade (ed.), *Six Contemporary British Novelists*. New York: Columbia University Press, 1976.

Todd, Richard. *Iris Murdoch: The Shakespearian Interest*. London: Vision, 1979. New York: Barnes & Noble, 1979.

Völker, Wolfram. *The Rhetoric of Love: Das Menschenbild und die Form des Romans bei Iris Murdoch*. Amsterdam: Grüner, 1978.

Wolfe, Peter. *The Disciplined Heart: Iris Murdoch and her Novels*. Columbia, Mo.: University of Missouri Press, 1966.

Zeigler, Heide, and Bigsby, Christopher (eds). *The Radical Imagination and the Liberal Tradition: Interviews with English and American Novelists*, pp. 209–30. London: Junction Books, 1982.

Articles and interviews

Bellamy, Frank O. 'An Interview with Iris Murdoch'. *Wisconsin Studies in Contemporary Literature*, 18 (1977), pp. 129–40.

Berthoff, Warner. 'Fortunes of the Novel: Muriel Spark and Iris Murdoch'. *Massachusetts Review*, 8 (1967), pp. 301–32.

Blow, Simon. 'An Interview with Iris Murdoch'. *Spectator*, 25 September 1976, pp. 24–5.

Bradbury, Malcolm. '"A House Fit for Free Characters": Iris Murdoch and *Under the Net*'. In *Possibilities: Essays on the State of the Novel*, pp. 231–46. London: Oxford University Press, 1973.

—— 'Iris Murdoch in Conversation with Malcolm Bradbury'. Recorded 27 February 1976, British Council tape no. RS 2001.

Bryden, Ronald. 'Talking to Iris Murdoch'. *The Listener*, 4 April 1968, pp. 433–4.

Byatt, A. S. Interview with Iris Murdoch on BBC programme 'Now Read On', 27 October 1971. (Unpublished.)

Conradi, Peter J. 'Useful Fictions: Iris Murdoch'. *Critical Quarterly*, 23, 3 (1981), pp. 63–9.

Davie, Gill. '"I should hate to be alive and not writing a novel": Iris Murdoch on Her Work'. *Woman's Journal*, October 1975.

Fletcher, John. 'Reading Beckett with Iris Murdoch's Eyes'. *AUMLA* (Australasian Universities Modern Language Association), 55 (May 1981), pp. 7–14.

—— 'Iris Murdoch'. Entry in Jay L. Halio (ed.), *Dictionary of Literary Biography*, Vol. 14 (*British Novelists Since 1960*). Part 2, pp. 546–61. Detroit, Mich.: Gale, 1983.

Fraser, G. S. 'Iris Murdoch: The Solidity of the Normal'. In John Wain (ed.), *International Literary Annual*, 2, pp. 37–54. London: Calder, 1959.

German, Howard. 'The Range of Allusion in the Novels of Iris Murdoch'. *Journal of Modern Literature*, 2 (1971), pp. 57–85.

Haffenden, John. 'In Conversation with Iris Murdoch'. *Literary Review/Quarto*, 58 (April 1983), pp. 31–4.

Harding, D. W. 'The Novels of Iris Murdoch'. *Oxford Magazine*, 26 October 1961, pp. 34ff.

Hayman, Ronald. 'Out of the Tutorial'. *The Times*, 30 September 1970. (On the opening of *The Servants and the Snow* at the Greenwich Theatre: interview with Iris Murdoch.)

Hebert, Hugh. 'The Iris Problem'. *The Guardian*, 24 October 1972. (On the opening of *The Three Arrows* at the Cambridge Arts Theatre: interview with Iris Murdoch.)

Heyd, Ruth Lake. 'An Interview with Iris Murdoch'. *University of Windsor Review*, 1 (1965), pp. 138–43.

Hobson, Harold. 'Lunch with Iris Murdoch'. *The Sunday Times*, 11 March 1962.

Hoffman, Frederick J. 'Iris Murdoch: The Reality of Persons'. *Critique: Studies in Modern Fiction*, 7 (Spring 1964), pp. 48–57.

—— 'The Miracle of Contingency: The Novels of Iris Murdoch'. *Shenandoah*, 17 (Autumn 1965), pp. 49–56.

Hope, Francis. 'The Novels of Iris Murdoch'. *London Magazine* (new series), 1 (August 1961), pp. 84–7. Repr. in Richard Kostelanetz (ed.), *On Contemporary Literature*, pp. 468–72. New York: Avon, 1964.

Kellman, S. G. 'Raising the Net: Iris Murdoch and the Tradition of the Self-Begetting Novel'. *English Studies*, 57 (1976), pp. 43–50.

Kermode, Frank. 'Novels of Iris Murdoch'. *Spectator*, 7 November 1958, p. 618.

—— 'The House of Fiction: Interviews with Seven English Novelists'. *Partisan Review*, 30 (1963), pp. 61–82. Repr. in Malcolm Bradbury (ed.), *The Novel Today*, pp. 111–35. London: Fontana/Collins, 1977.

—— 'Iris Murdoch'. In *Modern Essays*, pp. 261–6. London: Fontana/Collins, 1971.

McCarthy, Mary. 'Characters in Fiction'. *Partisan Review*, 28 (1961), pp. 171–91.

Maes-Jelinek, Hena. 'A House Fit for Free Characters: The Novels of Iris Murdoch'. *Revue des Langues Vivantes*, 39 (1963), pp. 45–69.

Magee, Bryan. 'Philosophy and Literature' (interview). In Bryan Magee (ed.), *Men of Ideas: Some Creators of Contemporary Philosophy*, pp. 262–84. London: BBC Publications, 1978.

Martin, Graham. 'Iris Murdoch and the Symbolist Novel'. *British Journal of Aesthetics*, 5 (1965), pp. 296–300.

Martz, Louis L. 'Iris Murdoch: The London Novels'. In Reuben A. Brower (ed.), *Twentieth-Century Literature in Retrospect*, pp. 65–86. Cambridge, Mass.: Harvard University Press, 1971.

Meidner, Olga M. 'The Progress of Iris Murdoch'. *English Studies in Africa*, 4 (March 1961), pp. 17–38.

Modern Fiction Studies, 15 (1969). Iris Murdoch Special Number. (Contains articles by Ann Culley, Linda Kuehl, Howard German, Raymond J. Porter, Alice P. Kenney, Peter Kemp, Frank Baldanza, William F. Hall, William M. Murray and a bibliography by Ann Culley, with John Feaster.)

Morrell, Roy. 'Iris Murdoch: The Early Novels'. *Critical Quarterly*, 3 (1967), pp. 272–82.

Nettell, Stephanie. 'Iris Murdoch: An Exclusive Interview'. *Books and Bookmen*, 11 (September 1966), pp. 14–15, 66.

O'Connor, William van. 'Iris Murdoch: The Formal

Contingent'. In *The New University Wits and the End of Modernism*, pp. 54–74. Carbondale, Ill.: Southern Illinois University Press, 1963.

Pearson, Gabriel. 'Iris Murdoch and the Romantic Novel'. *New Left Review*, 13–14 (January–April 1962), pp. 137–45.

Quinton, Anthony, *et al.* 'The New Novelists: An Enquiry'. *London Magazine* (old series), 5 (November 1958), pp. 13–31.

Ricks, Christopher. 'A Sort of Mystery Novel'. *New Statesman*, 22 October 1965, pp. 604–5.

Rose, W. K. 'Iris Murdoch, Informally'. *London Magazine* (new series), 8 (June 1968), pp. 59–73.

Rowe, Dilys. 'Sympathetic Fellow' (interview). *The Guardian*, 1 February 1960.

Sage, Lorna. 'In Pursuit of Imperfection'. *Critical Quarterly*, 19, 2 (1977), pp. 61–8.

——'Invasion of Outsiders'. *Granta*, 3 (1980), pp. 131–6.

Scholes, Robert. 'Iris Murdoch's *Unicorn*'. In *Fabulation and Metafiction*, pp. 56–74. Urbana and Chicago, Ill., and London: University of Illinois Press, 1979. (Originally published as *The Fabulators* (1967).)

Souvage, Jacques. 'The Unresolved Tension: An Interpretation of Iris Murdoch's *Under the Net*'. *Revue des Langues Vivantes*, 26 (1960), pp. 420–30.

—— 'Symbol as Narrative Device: An Interpretation of Iris Murdoch's *The Bell*'. *English Studies*, 43 (1962), pp. 81–96.

—— 'The Novels of Iris Murdoch'. *Studia Germanica Gandensia*, 4 (1962), pp. 225–52.

Sutcliffe, Tom. Interview with Iris Murdoch. *The Guardian*, 15 September 1980. (On the adaptation of *The Servants* as operatic libretto.)